HEALING

FROM

INFIDELITY

HEALING

FROM

INFIDELITY

The Divorce Busting®
Guide to Rebuilding Your
Marriage After an Affair

MICHELE WEINER-DAVIS

Michele Weiner-Davis Training Corporation

PO Box 1053

Woodstock, Illinois 60098

For information regarding Michele Weiner-
Davis, please contact her office

at 800-664-2435 or 303-444-7004

Email her at Michele@divorcebusting.com

Visit and sign up for Michele's newsletter at
www.healingfrominfidelity.com

Write to Michele Weiner-Davis

PO Box 271

Boulder, Colorado 80306

ISBN- 978-0-9980584-0-5

ISBN- 978-0-9980584-1-2

CONTENTS

ACKNOWLEDGMENTS

AS I REVIEWED my past writing, I noticed there has been a pattern to the acknowledgment sections in my previous seven books. My first expressions of gratitude have generally been focused on family, followed by friends, colleagues, editors, ending with an appreciation of the couples in my practice.

This time, I want to start off a bit differently- by acknowledging my immeasurable appreciation for the countless couples I've worked with over the years who were struggling with the fallout of an affair. You turned to me during the most vulnerable time in your lives, desperately searching for a helping hand.

From you, I have learned countless, invaluable lessons about what works and what doesn't work when trying to assuage pain from betrayal, rebuild trust and begin to love again. I have watched your reactions and responses with a careful eye, adjusting my approach as necessary to ensure that your marriage would heal… little by little….day by day. Without you as my living laboratory, I wouldn't have a sorely needed map to help couples repair their relationships after infidelity.

So, first and foremost, I want to thank all of you who believed in me and sensed that your marriage would be safe in my hands. I cherish the opportunities I have had to become intimately involved in your marriages, your families and in your healing journeys. Thank you from the bottom of my heart.

As always, on the top of my gratitude list, there's my family- my nearly life-long partner in everything- marriage, parenting, business and best friend, Jim, my daughter, Danielle, and my son, Zach, for encouraging, inspiring and most of all, *sustaining* me. You, and your loved ones (Dan, Little Taylor, Littler Reid and Jenna) make my life worth living. I don't know what I'd do without you.

I am also appreciative of the support I receive on many different levels from my devoted staff at The Divorce Busting® Center- my dear, old friend and assistant, Virginia, Cristy, and the Divorce Busting® coaches. Your dedication to our "marriage-saving mission" is remarkable and enduring. I am proud of you all. Thank you for your never-ending commitment to changing the world, one marriage at a time. In particular, I'd like to thank Virginia for her incredibly hard work in helping give birth to this book.

I'd also like to express gratitude to my wonderful friend and editor, Becky Johnson. I've been grateful for your presence in my life for a long time, but now I have another reason for my thankfulness; your editing brought clarity and depth to my writing. Thank you for your thoughtful, sensitive and creative contributions.

And last, but not least, I'd like to thank my close friends, both old and new, for making my life deliciously rich, so I feel replenished on Monday mornings when I walk into my office. You know who you are.

This book is dedicated to my amazing mother, talented therapist, and best friend, Elizabeth Weiner, who passed away suddenly and tragically in a car accident, and the new, little precious people in my life- my grandchildren, Taylor and Reid- who remind me of the ever-changing nature of life. I am truly blessed.

PART I

GETTING STARTED

CHAPTER ONE
INTRODUCTION

I T'S HAPPENED. THE last thing either you or your spouse could ever have imagined. One of you had an affair.

Perhaps you just discovered that your spouse has been unfaithful. Maybe you've been suspecting it for a while, but now you know for sure. You may have been innocently looking through some of your mate's belongings and found information that sent you reeling in shock and broke your heart. Or you might have been snooping for evidence because you've noticed some personality changes in your spouse. You've heard more excuses for being gone. And you've realized that he or she frequently leaves the room to check phone messages.

It's possible that your spouse finally decided to tell you about his or her actions because living a double life, the lying to someone they love, the loss of integrity... has become too painful to bear. Maybe someone else- a friend, an anonymous person, a family member, or even the affair partner, spilled the beans. In any case, the truth is out; your spouse has broken your marital vows and you can hardly breathe. The pain is unspeakable. You don't know which end is up.

No matter how suspicious you've been about the possibility that your partner may be straying, when suspicions of unfaithfulness are confirmed – it can send you reeling. Something deep inside you wants to believe that your spouse could never really, actually, break the sacred vow between you. Intimacy with anyone else? Unreal. Unthinkable.

Or perhaps you've discovered the truth, but your mind simply can't process what's happened. You feel like a person caught in a flood, your brain clinging to the driftwood of denial to avoid drowning in the rushing river of pain that comes with facing new and excruciating realities. "This can't possibly be happening to me. It can't be real. There must be some mistake. Maybe I'm reading too much into what I've discovered, allowing my imagination to run wild." But deep down inside, you know the truth. And now you have to deal with it. You feel caught in a nightmare from which you want to wake up. But it's not a nightmare. It's real. And it's really devastating. You're not sure what you want to do next. You're not even sure you can go on. For that matter, you're not sure about anything at all at the moment.

Or perhaps you're someone who found out about the infidelity a while ago and though the initial shock of discovery has passed, you feel like you're not functioning well. You're obsessed with thinking about the affair. "How could he do this to me,?" "Doesn't she know that this is the one thing I could never accept, a deal breaker?" "Was the other woman a better lover than I was?" "How could my wife love me and still sleep with another man?" The questions persist, in spite of all your best efforts to move on, and you feel no sense of peace or calm. You wish you could just turn back time and go back to the old you, the one who actually had a life. You can't believe you're still feeling so bad and so confused after all this time. You want help but you don't know where to turn.

At times, you want your spouse to comfort you. But often,

when she or he does, you feel resentful, angry and distraught. You don't want to be close. You can't act as though everything's okay when it's not. Your insides feel as though they've been whirled in a blender, and sometimes the emotional pain is so bad it physically hurts. By now, you thought you would be feeling better, but you're not. Shock may have turned to despair and what feels like chronic, low grade depression.

If this happens, it feels like you're stuck in a rut, or worse - a dark hole that often feels more like a grave. You just want to feel better! But you're losing hope that feeling normal and happy will ever be possible again. In short, my friend, you are grieving. Only there is no physical body to bury, no time-honored period of mourning, and no funeral. Something very precious and real has died; and yet you and your mate are still alive, breathing, moving through the days.

Whether you found out about the affair five minutes or a year ago, you may have a roller coaster of ambivalent feelings about whether or not to stay in your marriage. There are days when you are ready to call it quits and get an attorney, believing this might put an end to your misery. But when you think about what divorce really entails: ending your marriage, breaking up the family, splitting your finances, living alone, starting over from scratch— it gives you pause. You are living "in between trapezes," when life feels on hold, or suspended in mid-air between the Life You Knew and the Life to Come. This emotional space, between a rock and a hard place, is not only disorienting and sometimes crazy-making, it can hurt like hell.

Or perhaps you're the person who had the affair. The temptation was so great, the pull of secrecy so sensual – almost like a drug – that it may have felt impossible to resist. You didn't think beyond the thrill at hand. Your affair may have been an exciting break from a life you'd allowed to spiral into a boring routine. You wanted to feel the old spark, and to have an adventure, to feel alive. Or perhaps you were having marital problems, feeling discouraged, disillusioned and even feeling unheard or unseen, so you sought solace from someone other than your mate. It felt comforting and confirming. Or, your marriage may have been on firm ground, but the impulsive draw of doing something new, something fun or illicit in the moment, overwhelmed common sense and commitment.

But now your spouse knows about the affair, and all hell has broken loose. The last thing you wanted was to hurt him or her. And you certainly don't want a divorce. You had no idea that the fallout of your decision to be unfaithful would be so devastating. You have tried to help your spouse feel better, to assure them that what happened is over and in the past, but nothing you say seems to comfort them for long. They feel the anger and hurt all the time. Your whole relationship is focused on the infidelity. You understand why your spouse is in pain, but you could never have predicted that life as you knew it would be suspended; you never talk about anything else, you don't do anything fun together, there's always an undercurrent of anger or hurt. Your spouse's mood swings are palpable. You don't know what to do. It's not that you're unwilling to be supportive; it's just that anything you've tried doesn't seem to be effective.

You love your spouse and you want your marriage to work, but you are also beginning to wonder if she or he will ever be able to forgive you for straying. And although you understand why this is so, you worry that you'll spend the rest of your life repenting for your sins. When will it truly be "over," so you can live together in love and trust, the way it used to be, again? You don't want to spend the rest of your life and marriage in some emotional waiting room. You don't want to end your marriage but you're really at a loss. You wish there were a road map to help the two of you out of this adultery abyss.

Well, the good news is that there *is* a road map to help you both recover from infidelity and heal your marriage. And you happen to be reading it right now.

My name is Michele Weiner-Davis. I am the Founder of the Divorce Busting® Center in Boulder, Colorado and the website, www.healingfrominfidelity.com. I am also the best-selling author of seven other books including DIVORCE BUSTING and THE SEX-STARVED MARRIAGE. For more than 3 decades, I have been specializing in work with couples who are teetering on the brink of divorce. But it wasn't always that way.

Before my book, DIVORCE BUSTING was published, I was doing family therapy with adolescents and their families. During that time, I observed the toll that divorce took on the lives of families. It became obvious to me that divorce, except in the most severe cases such as ongoing physical abuse or addiction, created more problems than it solved. The ripple effect was devastating. I knew I had to do something about it.

I decided to write a book to help couples avoid divorce and keep their families together. When DIVORCE BUSTING was published, I was a lone voice; therapists are supposed to be neutral. The standard protocol was that a therapist should suspend any personal biases about the choices couples make to leave or stay in their marriage. A therapist should not voice his or her opinion, but rather draw out and support whatever the people involved in the marriage really wanted.

Without belaboring this issue, the truth is, when you go to a therapist, there is no way for that therapist's personal biases to be checked at the door. A therapist's values, beliefs and opinions about marriage and divorce always guide the sessions. So, in reality, there is no such thing as value-free therapy!

And since all therapy is value-laden, I felt the urgency to take a stand. I wanted to help couples find solutions to the problems they were facing so I decided to be bold and shout my decidedly biased "pro-marriage" opinion from the rooftops.

When the media learned about my counter-cultural and controversial book, I was invited to appear on every talk and news show imaginable including Oprah, The Today Show, 48 Hours, Good Morning America, 20/20, The Bill O'Reilly Show, and so on. My work was showcased in nearly every prominent newspaper and magazine as well. DIVORCE BUSTING became a best-seller.

As a result, requests for marital help came rolling in. I was so busy, I had to quit doing family therapy and narrow my focus to marriage-saving instead. This decision became a labor of love, a choice leading to what felt more like a meaningful, joyful calling than a job. The couples in my practice were learning relationship skills, putting aside their differences and reconciling their marriages. I was ecstatic.

During the last few decades where I've specialized in working with couples, I've learned an enormous amount about what it takes to make a marriage thrive. I've also learned a lot about what stressors place marriage at risk of divorce. And without question, I can tell you that infidelity is on top of a very short list of risk factors when it comes to rebuilding and sustaining loving, healthy marriages.

In my practice, I offer couples two-day intensives. They fly in from all over the world to work with me. And I would estimate that 85-90% of the couples in my practice are dealing with infidelity. I have been in the trenches with people whose lives have been turned upside down because of affairs. Because I'm determined to help people make their marriages work, I have developed a specific, doable and successful program for helping couples heal from infidelity and make their marriages strong again, and in fact, usually much stronger than the marriage was before the betrayal.

You may have heard the saying that, "We are stronger in broken places." In truth, when a bone breaks and then heals, the scar tissue is actually of stronger constitution than the bone itself. Eventually, a marriage can heal in the same way, and emerge even stronger in the broken places.

That said, healing from infidelity isn't easy. It's not for sissies. It's hard work. You have to be willing to do *whatever it takes* to turn things around. Sometimes, people have plenty of motivation to work on the relationship and to make things better but they just don't know how, they've no clue where to begin. And when what they've been doing isn't working, they feel like giving up, throwing in the proverbial towel of effort. Totally understandable. Look, if you haven't healed from infidelity before, how can you know what to do? Where to start? Finding a path out of the dark woods of despair is daunting.

That's where I come in. I have written this book because I want to walk you, *both of you,* step-by-step down the path to feeling better and more connected to each other. I want to help you put the infidelity in the past. I want to guide you toward rebuilding trust and confidence in one another and in your marriage. I want to share everything I've learned in the last few decades about how to navigate from the crisis of betrayal you are in, to loving each other completely again. I've done it for countless other couples over the years and now I want to do it for you. I'll coach you as if you were sitting in my therapy office!

This book is written for both you *and* your spouse. Although things between you are probably quite rough right now, I'm assuming that if you picked up or ordered and downloaded this book that you're both committed to working things out. I envision you working as a team and reading this book together. As you do, you'll notice that the book is organized in such a way that there are separate chapters for you and for your spouse. That said, I still want you to read each other's chapters. It's important that you both read the whole book so you can grasp the big picture, and get a vision for where we are going. Then you can go back and carefully re-read sections targeted for you, and apply the suggestions.

So, why are there separate chapters for each of you? Well, here's one of the tricky parts about recovery from an affair. Typically, each spouse is in a very different emotional place when they come for help. The person who has come clean about the affair usually is finally feeling better about being truthful and stepping into the light. They are ready to do the work. They just want me to tell them what to do.

On the other hand, what feels like "old news" to the spouse who had the affair, is very much "new news" to the betrayed partner and in fact, most feel they are at the lowest point in their lives when they come into my office. One person feels relieved and the other, devastated. Therefore, your journeys to feeling better are very different and require different interventions. Hence, the different chapters. But again, it's essential that you read *each other's* sections because there is information that will relate to you, and also help you understand what both of you need to heal and get back in a happier marriage groove. Okay?

If, at the moment, your spouse is less committed than you to improving things in your marriage, I've devoted two chapters to help you figure out what you need to do to improve things singlehandedly. Eventually, you will need each other's support to truly heal from betrayal. But in the meantime, there are things you can do- or stop doing- to enhance the chances of a positive outcome for your relationship.

Here's something else you should know before you get started. No matter how badly you might be feeling now, I promise your feelings will change. When you're going through a tough time, it's hard to imagine that you're ever going to feel differently, but you will. If you follow the steps outlined in this book, bit by bit, little by little, you will begin to feel lighter and more optimistic about the future. Here's what one client had to say about my program for helping couples heal from infidelity:

> After I found out about my husband's affair, I wanted to walk away. We tried years of "traditional" therapy and still, we were going nowhere. I thought I was ready to give up and move on, but I knew deep down inside it wasn't what I really wanted for myself, or my family.
>
> Then we decided to see Michele to give it one last ditch effort. Addiction, infidelity, and zero trust were the core ingredients that made up our recipe for disaster.
>
> We focused on what we needed to do to move forward, and learned how to effectively communicate. Wow, what a transformation! Not only did we not divorce, but we have been "honeymooning" since. That was several years ago. The word "divorce" has never been spoken in our household again! Thank you, Michele, for the direction and focus to put our lives back together!

Here's what another client said about my method of helping couples heal from infidelity:

> Our marriage was shattered by an affair. My wife and I decided immediately after the discovery of the affair that we both wanted to try to save the marriage.
>
> Unfortunately, neither one of us really knew what to do next. We did what most people do. We hired a 'marriage counselor' in our hometown. While I am sure that there are some great local marriage counselors out there, our

experience with our local counselor nearly destroyed the already fragile marriage my wife and I had left.

Here we were doing everything our counselor was telling us to do, yet nothing was getting better at home. We were talking about the marriage and our problems a lot; but nothing changed. It was starting to feel as if our marriage couldn't be saved. Our counselor finally advised that we needed to face the possibility that divorce may be the best option. It was devastating.

Michele was our last hope. I found Michele on the internet during a 'this can't be over' search for help. I was skeptical that anything or anyone could help but I couldn't give up. I didn't want to give up.

My wife and I spent two days with Michele in October. She helped us make a tangible, solution-focused plan to save our marriage. We did the work and I can honestly say that our marriage is better than it has been except for maybe the honeymoon phase we enjoyed 17 years ago. I will forever be grateful to Michele.

The shrapnel from the affair isn't gone. We still both hurt and will be dealing with the scars of the affair for a long time; but we have hope. We have confidence. We have each other. Michele helped us change the course of our marriage and because of that, our future, our two daughters' futures, and hopefully many generations to follow futures. My heartfelt prayer for you if you're reading this, is that your future can be changed too.

A 'thank you' to Michele feels so inadequate. I can only hope that these words will help you open your heart to believe that Michele can help you too.

So, now it's your turn. You don't have to struggle any longer. I am here to lead the way. I'll take the mystery out of putting the pain in the past. I will teach you what you need to know to create a new, more loving marriage with each other. Care to join me? Here's a sneak preview of what's to come.

In Chapter 2, "Boosting Your Infidelity I.Q.," - you will get answers to the most commonly asked questions about affairs such as, "My spouse and I disagree about the meaning of betrayal. So, what is betrayal,?" "How long does it take to heal,?" "Should we talk about the affair or not,?" "Should I discuss the affair with friends and family,?" and "What if I feel hopeless about my marriage,?" and many more.

Chapter 3, "Tasks for the Betrayed Spouse," outlines the preliminary steps to get your life on an even keel. Your whole world has been turned upside down and you need compassionate, honest direction and support to begin feeling better. This chapter will teach you specific, doable tasks and skills that will relieve much of your grief and pain. You'll learn how to decide whether or not to ask detailed questions about the affair. You'll learn how to help your spouse understand the depth of your despair. You'll put an end to destructive ways of interacting about what happened. You'll discover methods for coping with intense mood swings.

Chapter 4, "The Unfaithful Spouse's Tasks," offers concrete suggestions for the partner who had the affair. It describes the important initial steps you need to take to begin to heal, and also help your husband or wife to heal as well.

You are undoubtedly hurting too. You may feel lost and overwhelmed. Even with the best of intentions, your efforts to repair your marriage and feel better may be failing miserably. If you haven't yet ended the affair, you'll be given specific feedback about how exactly to say goodbye. And if you've had a difficult time dealing with your own moods, you'll better understand why this is happening. I'll help you figure out what you should or shouldn't share with your spouse about the betrayal. You will learn the best ways to be emotionally available to your spouse, even when it is hard. You'll receive tools to help you demonstrate the sincere remorse and regret you feel that will really make a difference to your partner. And finally, you'll gain some insight into the possible reasons you've strayed so you can avoid any temptation in the future.

Chapter 5, "Rebuilding: More Tasks for the Betrayed Spouse," outlines what you need to do when the worst of the initial crisis period is over. Although things are a bit better, the information in this chapter will help you feel more trusting and emotionally connected to your spouse.

In this chapter, you will also get help in identifying exactly what changes need to be made in your marriage to get it on solid, "affair-proof" ground. You'll get tips on how to better communicate your needs to your partner and learn what it means to do real giving in your relationship.

Additionally, you'll discover the power of positive reinforcement and the importance of empathy. Looping, intrusive thoughts usually go along with discovering an affair and each time you go down the same mental path, it hurts and slows down healing. I'll share a helpful strategy for eliminating those intrusive, obsessive thoughts that can so easily sabotage a good day and forward progress. Finally, healing involves personal work: steps you must take on your own to restore your self-esteem and belief in yourself. I'll help you do that.

In Chapter 6, "Rebuilding: More Tasks for the Unfaithful Spouse," you will identify specifically, how you'd like your marriage to be different. You'll investigate what, for example, would make you feel happier and more alive? I'll help you create a vision for a new, improved and healthier marriage. Also, I'll offer tools for avoiding triggers that might lead to unhealthy choices down the road. You'll be encouraged to talk with your spouse in ways that will inspire confidence in a brighter future. If you have lingering sadness or grief about the affair, I'll offer tips for working through this stage. Lastly, because you deserve it, if you haven't already done this, I will walk you down a path to forgiving and loving yourself.

Chapter 7, "Becoming Sexual Again," will offer you both guidelines for revitalizing this very important part of your relationship. Sometimes people start having sex right after the discovery of infidelity and other times, it feels nearly impossible to break the ice and be intimate again. This chapter will help you figure out what you need to do to feel sensually connected again. And if you're still having trouble dealing with the demons in your head, you'll learn some ways to work through this together.

Chapter 8, "When Your Spouse Won't End the Affair," is designed to give you a plan to save your marriage even though your partner may be ambivalent and unwilling to end the affair. If your spouse is not committed to working on the marriage, many of the strategies outlined in this book need to be tweaked, and I'll share which ones, and how to apply them in your particular situation. You'll need to be strategic in how you approach him or her. You'll also need emotional support because of the huge amount of patience that's required while your spouse sorts things out. This chapter will offer you that support.

In Chapter 9, "When Your Betrayed Spouse Wants Out," you'll discover some of the primary reasons a partner may feel they want to end the marriage during this process. But more importantly, you'll receive concrete suggestions for ways to approach your spouse to increase the odds that he or she will reconsider and reconcile.

Unfortunately, many of the things people do (often called, "what comes naturally") when their spouses are threatening to leave only make matters worse. I'll pinpoint these unhelpful actions and tell you what to do instead- actions that will serve you and your goals much better. I've developed a program called, The Last Resort Technique that will help you turn things around, even at the 11th hour.

Chapter 10, "Ten Tips for Affair Proofing your Marriage," will outline field tested strategies for strengthening your marriage and providing "love insurance" for the future. You'll learn 10 tips to insure that your marriage will stay strong, and that you're both "all in" and fully committed to a future together.

In Chapter 11, "Parting Thoughts," you'll read my final reflections about our journey together.

So, let's get started! I'm thrilled you're on the path to healing. I'm delighted to be walking with you down this road. Take your time. Go slowly. Take my advice to heart because I know it works. Countless others before you have moved from pain to loving again. I know you can do it too. I'll show you the way.

CHAPTER TWO
BOOSTING YOUR INFIDELITY IQ

TO GET YOU started on your healing journey, in this chapter, I will share with you some general thoughts and common questions about infidelity. The information in this chapter will lay the groundwork for the how-to chapters that follow. So, don't skip to Chapter 3. Take your time. In the end, it will speed things up. It will improve your infidelity I.Q.

What is betrayal?

Have you ever wondered what actually constitutes betrayal in a relationship? Do you and your spouse argue about the definition of it?

In the years that I have worked with couples, I've noticed great variation in what different people considered to be a betrayal. For some, betrayal means having an intimate conversation with a person of the opposite sex. For others, it's sexual intercourse. And for still others, it's everything in between: flirting, a too-familiar text, a hug or kiss, a series of late night phone calls.

So, what do you do when you and your partner's definitions are different? What should happen when one spouse believes they've been betrayed and the other disagrees?

I'll make it simple for you. In my opinion, I believe that betrayal is in the eye of the beholder. But what does this mean?

In the three decades that I've been working with couples, I've learned one important fact: relationships have to feel safe in order for intimacy to flourish. You must feel that your spouse is dependable, reliable, trustworthy, and transparent to allow yourself to be truly vulnerable. If something your partner does feels threatening to you, it hurts and destabilizes your relationship. When this happens, you are likely to protect yourself by shutting down emotionally or getting angry, neither of which lends itself to feelings of closeness and connection.

That's why it really helps for you and your partner to be clear about what, in your mind, constitutes a betrayal. What would it take for you to feel that your partner has truly gone beyond the boundaries of what feels comfortable and safe? If your line in the sand is different from your spouse's, you should honor their feelings. Let's say, for example, that your spouse doesn't want you to have intimate conversations about your marriage with a co-worker but you see nothing wrong with it. In this case, it's my strong belief that "intimate conversations with co-workers" should then be avoided in order to honor your mate's feelings, regardless of how you feel.

Similarly, if you don't want your wife going out drinking with single friends who like to dance with other men, but your wife thinks it's harmless, your wife needs to care enough about your feelings and find other ways to enjoy her free time.

In short, in marriage, it's reasonable to negotiate what works and what doesn't, but in the end, if there isn't a consensus, we must take care of our partner's feelings. Especially when it comes to choices we make that send red flags to our mate's feelings of safety and security in marriage. Good marriages are based on mutual caretaking. And if a particular behavior appears to be a slippery slope to one of you, if it is creating problems in the marriage, then this behavior should be re-evaluated. Let me give you an example of what I mean by a slippery slope.

Many married people believe it is fine to have a close friend of the opposite sex, but even this can become a slippery slope. A completely innocent meeting after work with co-workers may result in two people becoming excited about a project they will work on together. Research has shown that when we get caught up in an exciting new project, it produces dopamine in our brain. And sometimes the passion for the project crosses over into passion for the person who is working with you on this meaningful or exciting venture.

Co-workers, thus involved, can end up spending a great deal of time collaborating at work and the relationship becomes increasingly comfortable and familiar. Soon, they start having lunches together and when the work load increases, there are more demands on their time in order to complete the project. They work longer hours and may end up going out to dinner frequently.

Eventually conversations shift from business to life outside work. Over time, these talks get more and more personal. Occasionally, people discover that they can talk about certain subjects with their co-worker that they shy away from discussing with their spouses. A personal bond begins to form.

Shortly thereafter, conversations become even more intimate. Frequently, dissatisfaction about one's own marriage gets discussed.

Co-workers-turned-friends now commiserate and validate each other's feelings and become confidantes. Their communication defines their relationship as special and separate from each other's marriage.

The relationship may get physical at this point. But even if it doesn't, the real nature of the relationship is kept secret. And let me say this plainly: secrets place marriages at risk of divorce.

As you can see from this classic example of how affairs begin, the relationship started out completely innocently. But their small daily choices, though benign on the surface, lead to a connection that now threatens their marriages. Friends with benefits are not marriage-friendly.

If you still have questions about what constitutes a deception, ask yourself, "How would I feel if I were saying or doing this and my spouse were standing beside me?" Would you feel comfortable? Or would it feel awkward? Would you feel guilty? If the answer is "awkward" or "guilty," then you are involved in some form of betrayal. The "if-my-spouse-were-standing-there" yardstick is, in my opinion, a great self-test. It is important that you and your spouse agree on this yardstick moving forward.

Affairs are destructive in marriages

Some of my colleagues believe that Americans are too parochial in their views of infidelity and that we should be more accepting of adultery, the way other foreign cultures might be. In a recent study, 47% of the French population stated that it is immoral for a married person to have an affair. Compare that to 84% of Americans who believe extramarital affairs are morally wrong. Some believe that infidelity is not really the issue, it is that our culture has *unrealistic views* about marriage and monogamy.

But here's my perspective on this matter.

We don't live in those countries. We live here. And our expectations, feelings, thoughts are all shaped by our culture. Because this is so, I can tell you first-hand from working with couples in the trenches what it's like when infidelity has just been discovered.

The betrayed spouse feels absolutely devastated beyond words. She or he feels as if the whole world has turned upside down. The ground that felt solid beneath them is shaking and they begin not just to question the affair, but a dozen other "realities" they had trusted in the marriage. An affair creates a domino effect, leaving the betrayed spouse wondering, "What is true,?" and "What is real?" So many people truly believe that their spouses would never, ever stray and when they do, betrayed spouses feel a sense of altered reality and general disorientation. Anxiety and depression set in.

I had a woman in my practice recently who had lost all four of her immediate family members. Her 25-year old sister died from breast cancer. Her mother had a brain tumor. Her father died of a heart attack shortly thereafter. Then her brother died in a car accident. She added that she had two miscarriages in the process. So much loss, enough to do anyone in. But she was incredibly strong. In fact, I'd say she was amazing.

Then she started to talk about finding out that her husband had an affair. She began to cry and said, "Finding out that he had an affair was *the* defining moment of my life. I will never be the same. This affair defines me."

I could hardly believe that after all this brave woman had survived, she was telling me that her husband's affair was so horrific that "it defined" her as a person. The affair had not only caused her grief, she felt it had shattered her very identity at the core of her being.

I was quick to remind her that the affair didn't define her, or anyone for that matter. What defined her was her resilience. In her mind, four deaths of close family members didn't begin to touch the kind of pain she was experiencing after learning of her husband's betrayal. In some ways, death is easier.

I will tell you a lot more about this in the next chapter, but suffice it to say, that when the crisis of infidelity strikes a marriage, the person who has been betrayed may show symptoms similar to those found in post-traumatic stress. They feel violated and can hardly function. Trust, which is the very foundation of marriage, needs to be restored and this is no simple task. I've said it before and I'll repeat it again and again: healing from infidelity is hard work.

I don't want you to feel discouraged however. Though getting your marriage back on track is challenging, it is a sure-fire outcome if you both follow the steps outlined in this book. I simply want you to understand that if you've been feeling crappy, crazy, disoriented and a little detached from reality, there's a good reason for it; your marriage has taken a hit.

But as you know, how *you handle* what life throws your way makes all the difference in the world. A friend of mine once said, "What happens in life is less important than what happens next." Although you've been going through one of the roughest times in your marriage, you can (and will) come out the other side. In fact, many clients have shared that had it not been for their partner's affair, they'd never have looked at, discussed, and healed some of the underlying issues that were broken at the foundation of their relationship. Their marriage would have remained on auto-pilot. In other words, the affair acted as a powerful catalyst to marital change for the better.

Can you really bounce back and heal from an affair? Can you feel better? Can your marriage be even stronger? Absolutely. I've worked with countless couples who have decided to divorce their old marriages and start new ones with each other, ones that are more honest, loving and passionate. But the only people who get to that point are the courageous, hard-working couples who are committed to doing *whatever it takes.*

Though infidelity is a serious breach of marital commitment, it is not, by any means, a marital deal breaker. When you are tempted to think all is lost, keep this in mind. You would be surprised how many couples have survived an infidelity, healed and moved on to a deeper, more authentic and passionate marriage.

How long does it take to heal?

I need to give you a heads up. Throughout this book, you will hear me use the phrase, "That depends." If you want to know how long it will take for your marriage to truly be in good shape, I will tell you, "That depends." Why? Because people and relationships are unique. No two marriages are the same. No two acts of betrayal are identical. Every spouse working this program will have different personal strengths and weaknesses. Some people will find their relationship has normalized, and even improved within a few months. For others, it may take years.

But I *can* tell you a few things about the healing process. First of all, for most people, it takes a good long while for the pain to diminish. In the beginning, the betrayed spouse is often consumed with thoughts about the affair and the pain is overwhelming. Over time and with work, "the bad thoughts" happen less frequently and when they pop up, they don't create the same sting as they did months before. Eventually, thoughts of betrayal fade into the background and are replaced with an increased and proactive focus on forgiveness and emotional and physical connection.

However, you can't rush the process. It is what it is. Regardless of what you're feeling, you have to remind yourself that this is a process which takes time and in the end, everything will feel better. You have to trust the process. You may have heard the saying, "In the end, it will all get better. And if it is not better, it is not the end." In my years of living and working with others, I've found this to be profoundly true.

But I know that asking you to believe things will get better, right now, this moment, may be a huge leap of faith because you just aren't feeling hopeful. There are intense ups and downs in this journey. Lots of them. There will be times when you sense real improvements and you start saying to yourself, "We're getting better. Things are moving in the right direction." And then, with one incident or painful trigger, it all comes tumbling down. You and your spouse go out to dinner, you're having a great time, and all of a sudden you notice that the waitress's name is Sandy, and Sandy is the name of your husband's affair partner. Not only does the dinner go downhill, the following week you and your spouse barely speak to each other.

Or similarly, just when you feel you and your spouse are becoming closer, you can't stop the private looping reel of images or excruciating thoughts in your head. You envision the other guy and your wife together at the hotel and you keep wrestling with thoughts such as, "Is he a better lover than me?" "Did she do sexual things with him that she's never done with me?" And before you know it, you feel like you're back to square one.

Often, just when you think you've turned a corner, the negative self-talk comes creeping in, sabotaging any positive changes- "I don't want him to think everything is okay, when it isn't. I can't believe I'm putting up with this in my life!" Or, "How could she have done this to me? She couldn't possibly love me if she made the choice to screw some other man." Unbridled anger brings the progress to a screeching halt. I will help you understand and manage leftover or reoccurring anger, and teach you how to direct your emotions in ways that are productive and helpful.

Many betrayed partners feel that their unfaithful spouse should bend over backwards to make life better, as a sort of penance for the pain they caused. So, any time he or she disappoints in some way- he doesn't pitch in with kids or cooking, she won't stop doing Facebook at night- it starts a rushing river of negative feelings. All flowing back to the ocean of The Affair.

So, the upshot is this. Healing from infidelity is *not* a straight line. It is a zigzagging journey that includes many, many ups and downs. You will be on a wild roller coaster, so you better buckle your seat belt. You have to expect these intense ups and downs. It goes with the territory.

Frequently, couples in my practice get very discouraged when they encounter a dip in the roller coaster. They start to ask themselves if what they're doing is really working. Are they just fooling themselves? They need constant reminders that what they're experiencing is completely normal and with time, the hills and valleys will level out.

As you read this book and put the tools I teach into practice, I guarantee that you too will experience these ups and downs. Embrace them. Learn from them. I will show you how.

Should we put the affair in the past and quit talking about it, or should we focus on it?

Janet and Mark sought my help because Mark had a 6-month long affair with a co-worker. Janet discovered intimate texts and late night phone calls and confronted Mark, who then told the truth about his actions. Janet felt absolutely devastated. She was obsessed with thoughts about Mark's affair and talked about it every day. She was deluged with questions and overwhelmingly painful feelings and simply couldn't think of anything else.

When we began our work together, Janet and Mark had a burning question for me. Mark understood that Janet would have some questions about what happened, but he couldn't believe how often she felt the need to discuss the affair. He wondered how it would be possible to mend their marriage if all they were doing was "picking the scab." It was Mark's belief that nothing heals if you keep rehashing the problem.

Janet, on the other hand, was furious that Mark was resistant to talking about the affair when she so desperately needed to do so. She felt there was no way she could heal if he wasn't willing to help her make sense of what happened. In fact, the more Mark dug in his heels about not wanting to focus on the past, the more Janet believed he had no idea of the depth of the pain he'd put her through, and she sincerely doubted that their marriage would ever get better. They wanted me to tell them who was right. Was it Janet, who needed to talk about the affair? Or Mark, for wanting to put the past in the past and leave it there?

My answer is simple; they were both right. As you'll learn in the next chapter, when the betrayed spouse has the need to talk about what happened and about feelings associated with the affair, healing will not occur unless these discussions take place. That said, there also needs to be problem-free times in the marriage; times when spouses declare a moratorium on "affair talk."

How much you're doing of each will depend on where you are in the process of healing. Early on, many couples find themselves doing marathon talk sessions. With time, these discussions become more limited.

In the next chapter, I will offer more specific guidelines to help you determine when talking is useful and when it can be destructive. But for now, if you and your partner have been arguing about who's right and who's wrong regarding talking about the affair versus moving on, know that it isn't either/or. It's both. You're both right.

Spending time together helps

In an attempt to help the betrayed spouse come out of the fog and feel less anxious and more connected to his or her partner, I routinely ask, "What's different about the times when you are feeling just a little bit better?" Hands down, the most common response is, "I feel okay when my spouse is with me, but as soon as she or he leaves my presence, things fall apart again. I can't stop wondering, feeling anxious and alone."

Needless to say, two people can't put their entire lives on hold forever, nor would that be a good idea, however, there is something magically reassuring about the physical presence of one's spouse when assurance of their love is so sorely needed. The importance of extended time together at this juncture of their lives — to talk, hold each other, cry, and just be — simply cannot be overstated.

This might mean taking time off from work or rearranging schedules. Although taking time off or re-structuring schedules may be inconvenient, it's essential. What are vacation days for anyway? Typically, people who avoid this step and try to pretend that, after the discovery of an affair, life is business as usual, have a more difficult and protracted healing process.

Given that the #1 cause for productivity problems at work is marriage and family problems, you might think that infidelity leave — where employees would be entitled to spend a few days with their grieving spouses, would be an extremely cost-effective policy.

That said, it may not be possible for you or your spouse to

arrange time off from work. If not, in the next chapter, I'll offer suggestions of ways to stay connected even if you're apart. Staying connected is key.

On the other hand, you might be someone who prefers being alone right now. You are dealing with a lot of emotions and it's possible that your spouse's presence feels a bit too overwhelming at the moment. If so, that's fine. Express your need for extra solitude. There is no single correct way to do this. Listen to your heart, trust your gut, and do what works best for you.

I need support. Is it a good idea to talk to family and friends about the affair?

You have been so distraught about the affair; you need a shoulder to lean on. But you have to be careful about whom you choose to be your confidantes. Let me explain why.

In all likelihood, your natural instinct is to turn to friends and family, the people closest to you. You tell them about the problems in your marriage. Support and empathy is what you're after.

The advice you get feels right. They say things that soothe you and justify your anger. "I can't believe your husband treats you that way. You shouldn't put up with it." Or, "Your wife doesn't deserve you. You are so good to her and she is so self-absorbed." Vindicated and bolstered, you leave these conversations feeling better. "You're right," they say, and "your spouse is wrong." That feels good.

Eventually, you are regularly being urged to cut your losses and get out of your marriage. Your friends and family can't stand to see you hurt any longer. They want you to get on with your life. "Enough is enough," they tell you, and may suggest you see a divorce attorney. And as you're about to see, while it may feel comforting to know that there are people who love, support and understand you, relying on family and friends in this way can easily backfire.

What happens if, for a variety of reasons (the kids, your history together, your financial situation, a deep abiding love), you decide you want to work on your marriage in earnest? Ideally, you'd like to stay together. Then what?

You suddenly learn that your inner circle is not impressed. They're not happy, far from it. They're skeptical and filled with contempt toward your straying spouse.

They tell you, "Can't you see that he's just trying to manipulate you?" "She's on her best behavior, but it won't last." "Once a cheater/liar, always a cheater/liar." "You've been wanting to get out of your marriage and now you are being brainwashed to stay."

They're frustrated and angry because you've leaned on them and basked in their emotional support, and now that time has passed and emotions are settling down, you see things a bit more clearly. You want to stay married and work things out!! But to others who don't love your mate, who don't know all the intricacies in your relationship, your choice to stay seems simply unacceptable.

So, you try to explain that things are different now. You give examples of all the thoughtful things your spouse is doing to show he or she cares. But your friends and family won't budge. You just don't understand why they're so stubbornly clinging to their negative views of your mate. Why aren't they happy for you? Why aren't they delighted that your marriage has turned a corner? Why don't they see the changes in your spouse?

And if they really loved you, regardless of what they think about your spouse, shouldn't they just want you to be happy, even if they don't agree with your decisions?

I was deeply saddened by a situation much like the one I just described, just this week. A couple married for 10 years with two young children sought my help. The wife was desperately unhappy because her husband, a workaholic, had been emotionally distant, uninvolved with the children, critical and demeaning. Because of her unhappiness, she spent extended periods of time with her parents and siblings who lived out of town.

Her husband felt neglected, lonely and unappreciated. Rather than discuss their feelings openly and honestly, they argued and retreated to separate quarters. Instead of being intimate partners, they were more like toddlers engaging in parallel play.

To satisfy a deep void from within, the husband turned to sex outside the marriage: lots of it. He found himself in a web of sexually compulsive behavior. His wife, though emotionally detached, sensed something was not right and began sleuthing to catch him. She solicited help from computer-savvy relatives and within a short period of time, got all the information she needed to make a decision about her marriage. She wanted out. Her siblings cheered her on and the once-adored husband, brother and son-in-law got slapped with the scarlet letter. He was ostracized from a family he dearly loved.

The wife sought legal advice and announced her intentions to divorce her husband. He was crushed and begged her to come for a two-day intensive with me. As is often the case with these challenging but productive intensives, this couple decided to tackle the issues that led them astray and recommit to working on their marriage rather than to divorce. Though well aware that the road to recovery would be fraught with challenges and hard work; nonetheless, a feeling of optimism was palpable in my office.

Until they went back home.

Upon hearing the news of possible reconciliation, this woman's family was livid, and showed their outrage. Her brothers and sisters vacillated between refusing to talk to her and non-stop, harassing telephone calls. As weeks passed, in spite of the impressive, heartfelt, and profoundly life-transforming work these two individuals had been doing on themselves and their marriage, her family hadn't been swayed. Dealing with complicated and painful marital issues was tough enough for this young wife. Working through the detailed disclosure about his sexually compulsive behavior was a huge challenge. Now, this. While she was doing the hard work of reconciliation, she felt she had to defend her husband and fight off hateful interference from those she'd trusted with her pain.

Through tears, they told me about her family's hurtful reaction. Although I'm hopeful her family will eventually come around, my heart ached for them. But I was not surprised. I've seen this dynamic many times.

So, here's some advice.

If you're having a hard time, it's reasonable to assume that you will want to discuss your situation with people closest to you-good friends and relatives. Understand that when you do, they will naturally take your side. The more information you share about your spouse's "wrongdoings," the more your friends and family will object to his or her presence in your life. They want to protect you.

If you sense that your loved ones are becoming biased, it's wise to limit complaints about your marriage and consult with a therapist instead. Make sure you hire a marriage-friendly therapist. Don't expect your family to be able to readily switch gears about your spouse's potential to change just because you have. They may just need more time than you do to trust that the changes are sincere, and lasting. Whatever you do, while they catch up to you, don't allow their pessimism to thwart your marriage-saving plans.

Hopelessness is the real cancer in marriage

In all the years I've been helping couples heal from infidelity, I can tell you that there's only one time when I start to worry about the fate of their marriage. It's when one or both of the partners start to become hopeless. Although I completely understand why there are points in the process where the problems seem insurmountable; hopelessness about the viability of the marriage can thwart all the positive efforts to turn things around.

Everyone knows about the importance of having a positive attitude in life in general. People with positive attitudes are healthier, both physically and mentally. They are also happier. But a positive attitude is even more crucial when working on overcoming considerable marital problems. A positive or hopeful perspective can mean the difference between making your marriage work and having it fail.

And this attitude needs to come, eventually, from both of you. One positive partner, alone, can't drag a negative, hopeless spouse into a happy, healthy marriage. Ultimately, this process will take two hopeful partners to move into a more loving and happier place.

There is extensive research about the power of optimism and hope when trying to heal from illnesses, particularly life threatening ones. Many people have recovered from serious life-threatening diseases through good medical care *and* working hard on themselves to expect positive outcomes. There is a saying, "Seeing is believing," but I also think the opposite is true; "Believing is seeing." In other words, when you both create a positive vision for your marriage and expect the best from each other, it actually increases the chances you'll achieve your goals.

I want you to know about the countless couples I've worked with over the years, couples who weren't at all certain that they could muster the strength to work things out. They had many dark times. But with my program, they were able to rebuild their love and trust and stay married. And they didn't just endure an unhappy, "intact marriage," they worked for and got an "intimate, loving marriage."

Couples with children were also able to give their children a gift of a lifetime: working things out when things got tough. Resiliency is an amazing life skill for children to learn and to bring into their future lives as adults. If you have children, they will have both of you to thank for this precious gift of persevering through life's inevitable rough patches.

Since you are reading this, I know you have hope and that you're motivated. I also know that your hope will dip from time to time. But I want you to know that when you're feeling doubtful, pessimistic or wanting to throw in the towel, I will be your reservoir of hope. I will remind you that your mood swings are normal and that you can and will come out the other side.

You and your spouse might take turns being hopeful about your marriage; when you feel up, your spouse might feel down, or visa verse. That's totally normal too. It's important that one of you remembers that you will soon begin to see some light. And that light will lead the way.

As the late Robert Schuller once said, "Let your hopes, not your hurts, shape your future."

PART II

GETTING THROUGH THE CRISIS

CHAPTER THREE

THE BETRAYED SPOUSE'S TASKS

A LTHOUGH THIS BOOK will help couples heal from infidelity together, both you and your spouse have your own individual work to do as well. If you've read this far, I know you are ready. It's time to push up your sleeves and begin the hard work of recovering from pain and piecing your life back together again. It won't be easy, but when you invest in this process, you will start to feel more connected to your spouse, helping you feel better in general, and before long, you'll be as convinced as I am that the work is well worth the effort.

Before I describe what you need to do step-by-step, I want to remind you to be gentle with yourself. Don't judge yourself if you're having a bad day and you fail to follow the steps outlined. We all have bad days from time to time. I will help you figure out what you need to do to turn a bad day into a better one. Also, fight back the temptation to make overly ambitious goals. If you do, you will surely be disappointed. In fact, before I give you information about the tasks that lie before you, I want to help you set a few reasonable goals for yourself. Let's start now.

1. On a 1-10 scale, with 1 being, "I feel terrible" and 10 being "I feel great," how would you rank your feelings, overall, in the last week or so?

2. Given that no one ever feels great all the time, where on the 1-10 scale would you need to be to feel satisfied?

3. What would be one or two small things that could happen or that you could do in the next week or so to move you up half a point from the response you gave in question #1?

For example, if you said that you've been feeling about a "2" on the scale, what would have to happen for you to feel you've moved up to a "2 ½" or a "3?" For instance, if you've been crying for several hours each day, but this week you were to go one full day without crying, perhaps you'd evaluate yourself at a "2 ½" or a "3." Every small improvement is progress.

As you think about your response, make sure your answer is both concrete and action-oriented. Don't just say, "I will *feel* better," or "I will be sleeping better." What will you be *doing* when you are feeling better? Will you start exercising again, go back to work, be able to eat meals? What will be the first behavioral sign that you are feeling better? In other words, ask yourself, "What action can I imagine myself *doing* that would help me note a slight improvement,?" rather than, "What will I be *feeling*?"

Similarly, how will you know if you are sleeping better? Will you sleep for a couple of hours instead of not at all? Will you wake up only two times in the middle of the night instead of every half hour? Be as specific as you can possibly be.

Secondly, make absolutely certain you aren't expecting too

much of yourself as you look for signs of improvement. Be sure you are anticipating reasonable goals, baby steps forward. Try to set small goals that could realistically, conceivably happen within a week's time. Would it be possible for someone who'd been crying "all the time," to go a full day without crying at all, within a week's time? For most, I would say, yes, that's a doable change.

On the other hand, if you happen to be crying every day and you expect the first sign of change will be that you'll stop shedding any tears at all, you'll likely be disappointed and feel discouraged. Err on the side of caution. Expect less of yourself, knowing that change takes time. Then when you meet one small, doable goal, you will feel good about your progress. Remember, the road to healing is one small step at a time. Begin by defining your "small, observable, measurable" goal. When you are *doing* something different (a concrete action), it takes you one little step closer to healing. Inch by inch.

Here are a few more examples of action-oriented goals.

- I will be getting dressed for the day as soon as I finish breakfast, rather than waiting until noon.

- I will write a list of three simple tasks to do each day and accomplish at least two out of three.

- I will make myself a nourishing meal for dinner rather than eat nothing all day.

- I will make a plan to get together with a friend one day this week even though I might not feel like it.

As you read through the steps in this chapter, you'll come to understand that recovering from such a deep blow to the heart is a process not unlike recovering from a car accident or major surgery, and sometimes a much slower process than you want it to be.

But good, deep healing simply takes time. If you had been in a physical accident, you would have EMT's arrive at the scene and begin life-stabilizing emergency treatment before they carried you off in an ambulance to the hospital, for the next stages of treatment and healing.

This chapter is the emotional equivalent to what an EMT would do for you. When I am the "first responder" to a spouse in the throes of learning about their mate's affair, I begin by offering these initial thoughts and suggestions to help stabilize a newly broken heart that is often still reeling from shock. In Chapter 5, I'll be outlining steps you will take later in the process of healing, once you are a little less emotionally raw.

Begin by reading slowly through this chapter. (Even reading and comprehension can slow down while you are in emotional overwhelm.) Since no two people are exactly alike, I can't give you a precise timeline for how fast you work through this program. Move at your own rate. Do what feels comfortable for you at first. There may be a time when you need to give yourself a little nudge to follow through on a task; but especially in the beginning, take things slowly. Are you ready?

Know that whatever you're thinking and feeling is normal

If you recently found out that your spouse has had an affair, chances are you are incredibly emotionally distraught.

Here's what I would do if you walked into my office, feeling disoriented and devastated after learning about your spouse's unfaithfulness. After getting you seated and comfortable, offering you a cup of tea, I'd want to know how you're doing. And when you'd tell me how awful your life has been, I might share what are absolutely normal responses to an emotional shock.

I'd tell you that you might not be able to think straight. You may be crying a great deal. You may be sleep deprived. Your appetite might be totally gone or you may find yourself eating comfort foods throughout the day. You may feel enraged one minute and devastated the next. Perhaps you find it impossible to concentrate. You may not be able to focus at work (if you are even able to go back to work) and you may struggle with taking care of your children.

After such betrayal, you will feel as though you can't escape constant, looping thoughts about the affair.

From the moment you wake up until the moment you go to sleep, the affair is first and foremost on your mind. And when you finally fall asleep, you have dreams about it. Or should I say, nightmares? You feel lost, disoriented, disconnected and devastated. You wonder if you will ever feel okay again.

Some days, you question your sanity. At times, you may feel detached from reality because you are living in your head, which is overwhelmed with a dizzying cocktail of emotions.

And when you're not feeling sad or depressed, you feel enraged. "How could my spouse do this to me,?" you wonder. You never, in a million years thought this could happen to you. "Not my spouse, not my marriage," has been your mantra. But now you find yourself in a place you never expected to be. You always thought you wouldn't put up with infidelity and here you are, in the middle of a trauma that you didn't see coming.

It's happened, but you don't want your marriage to end. Or do you? You are so angry that your life has taken this turn that there are days when you can't imagine staying with your partner. After all, if she or he could be unfaithful once, couldn't it happen again? Your head is swirling. You don't know which end is up. You just want it all to go away. And clearly, it isn't going away. You are so emotional, you just don't know how to begin calming yourself down.

If this sounds familiar to you, again I want you to hear me say: what you are experiencing is *completely and positively normal*. You aren't losing your mind. It's dreadful to have these thoughts and feelings, but they go with the territory when you discover infidelity. One of the reasons you feel so badly is because you care about your marriage so much, you can't believe this has actually happened. Your very identity and feelings of safety, once foundational to your well-being, have been shaken to the core.

In some ways, finding out about infidelity feels like learning about a death of a loved one. You are in shock. And you are grieving the loss of the dream you treasured of a loving marriage to a faithful partner. The lies, the deceit, the betrayal, all go a long way to destroy trust and hope. As you work through the pain of the betrayal, you will have to figure out a way to wrap your brain around the fact that this has happened in your lives. In other words, you will have to move to a place of acceptance. It will take time, but until you get there, inner peace is hard to come by.

It's very common for people to be in denial about the affair, even when they have the facts. When someone suddenly loses their spouse in an unexpected way, they often experience what author Joan Didion calls "magical thinking." Very simply, it takes our brains, so accustomed to our former life, a long while to dissemble old realities, and create new synapses, embracing such difficult new realities. Until then, especially in those first days and weeks after discovery, denial of reality and wishful thinking is common. The betrayed partner simply can't adjust to the fact that their marriage has been "tainted" forever. They find it difficult, if not impossible at first, to truly accept that infidelity is now part of their marital history, the story of their lives. But it is. And with time and genuine marital healing, people eventually find healthy ways to make peace with what's happened and move forward. I know that's hard for you to imagine right now.

And because acceptance is hard to imagine right now, you shouldn't spend too much time trying to do it.

Continue to gently remind yourself that the roller coaster of emotions, though distressing, is normal and natural. Just allow the feelings to be there without judgment. You will get through this and your feelings will change with time (and effort).

Once you understand that anything you feel right now is normal and look at yourself with kindness instead of judgment, what then?

Express your thoughts and feelings to your spouse

I've found that most people who have been betrayed find themselves wanting to talk about what they're feeling. And the research shows that if you have the need to talk about the affair and the havoc it's wreaked in your life, you must have an outlet for it. Your spouse needs to hear how his or her decisions have impacted on your life.

In this section, I will guide you as to the best way to share your feelings with your spouse, so that it is truly helpful.

Chances are, your spouse won't love hearing about your pain. There are lots of reasons for this- he or she feels devastated, guilty, _____ (fill in the blank) that you are hurt. But don't worry about that because I am going to address this directly in the following chapter devoted to your mate. You do your job, I'll do mine and your spouse will do theirs.

If your spouse has a difficult time listening, don't assume they don't care about your feelings. Sometimes when a person has been unfaithful, they feel so much shame that it's hard to listen to the pain they've inflicted. Instead of being empathetic, your spouse might just be defensive. But again, their "unwillingness" to listen is not necessarily an indication of not caring; it's often an indication of regret, shame, and guilt. Try to keep this in mind. If your mate's shame is preventing him or her from really listening to what is in your heart, it will thwart the healing process. But as I said, I will address this issue with your mate.

Timing is everything. It helps to set aside a specific time to talk about your feelings. If you have children, don't talk about what's happened in front of them. It is none of their business. Even if your children found out about the affair accidentally, avoid sharing your emotions about it with them. Talk to your spouse. It's an adult issue.

As tempting as it may be to unburden your heart, talking to your children about the affair only burdens them unnecessarily. Children need to be children. They're not there to take care of their parents' emotions. Plus, because you are feeling so low, it's quite likely that you will say things about your spouse that are derogatory, which in the long run, is emotionally damaging for your kids. It's unhealthy to expect children to take sides in situations like this. Take the high road. Talk to your spouse. Talk to safe friends and family. But leave your children out of this mess as much as possible.

Sometimes people say, "But my child is a teenager or a young adult. Can't she or he hear about the affair?" My advice remains the same. For now, work through this process with your partner, not your children. You can both agree that if the older kids ask, you can say something like, "We love you. And this is not a problem you need to worry about. We are getting expert help and as adults, can work through whatever issues need addressing in our marriage. Thanks for caring about us."

And while you're deciding who is safe to talk to about what

happened, re-read the section in Chapter 2 about the fallout of talking to well-meaning friends and family. For the best chance at repairing a marriage after an affair, you need to make sure that your confidantes are people who will support you to stay in your marriage despite what has happened, and despite the fact that you have been hurt. Confidantes need to be marriage-friendly and love both of you.

As challenging as it might be, the most important person with whom to share your feelings is your spouse. After years of helping couples talk about infidelity, I can tell you that, even under the best of circumstances, discussions about feelings of betrayal are very, very difficult. If you are able to do it productively, that's great. If you need a few guidelines to help you through it, here are some that my clients have found particularly helpful.

Express anger, but don't be intentionally hurtful.

While your spouse needs to know how hurt and angry you feel, it isn't helpful for you to shame him or her or become verbally abusive. I can guarantee that if your goal in "talking about the affair," is to hurt your spouse for hurting you, things will just go from bad to worse. Plus, your spouse will become defensive and you won't get the support you so desperately need and deserve. In fact, your spouse will begin to avoid any conversation about your feelings. You don't want this to happen.

Let me give you an example of a couple I worked with who needed guidance because the wife, Sandy, was so degrading when she told her husband, Sam how she felt about his affair.

"You should have just kept your dick in your pants instead of fucking that ugly whore,!" she vented, unleashing her rage. "But you couldn't do that, could you? And now everyone knows that you're an asshole and there must be something wrong with me for staying with a piece of shit like you."

Needless to say, Sam shut down completely.

Clearly, name-calling is off-limits. Derisive language is not okay. Contempt has no place in these discussions. I called Sandy on it. I told her that if she wants to let Sam know that she is furious about what he did, that she doesn't know if she'll be able to get through her anger, that's fine. She can even tell him that she feels enraged. But as I said, accusatory, hurtful language is unacceptable.

Furthermore, I told Sandy that I understood that she was very angry with Sam. "But frequently," I added, "anger is a smokescreen for hurt. I wonder if underneath all this rage there is really a boat load of hurt?" At this, Sandy began to cry. Soon her cries turned to heart-wrenching sobs. She told Sam how deeply hurt she was. Sam reached out to her and started rubbing her arm in a genuine gesture of comfort. Sandy much preferred his comforting her over his previous response of shutting down. Allowing yourself to show vulnerability will often yield better results.

So, when you want to talk about your feelings, give your spouse a heads up. Arrange a time to talk that is good for both of you. Before you speak, take a deep breath. Remember, the goal of these conversations is for you to air your feelings without putting down your spouse. Your spouse's choices don't have to steal your dignity, or make you react in ways that are beneath you. Taking the high road- refusing to be venomous out of spite—is a choice you will never regret when it comes to conversations about the affair.

If you sense you are not in a balanced emotional place to talk, that your feelings are just too raw and you fear erupting in a fit of rage – postpone the conversation until you can either get to a better place or have the initial conversations in the presence of a trusted therapist who can help keep emotions in check.

It helps for you to use "I-messages."

I-messages are statements you make where you take personal responsibility for your thoughts and feelings rather than blame or criticize your spouse. The statements often start with the word, "I." Let me give you some examples.

Instead of saying, "You really blew it. You ruined our marriage," say, "I feel like you made a huge mistake. There are times I feel like I'll never recover from this." Or, instead of saying, "You never care about my feelings, so why should this be any different,?" say, "I am devastated because it feels like I wasn't even on your radar when you met with (the affair partner) time and time again."

In other words, talk about how *you* feel, how *you* see things rather than diagnose or blame your spouse. Even though you might think that your spouse deserves blame, your talks will go considerably better if you just talk about what's in your heart and on your mind.

Naturally, there will be some talks that become inflammatory, even with the best of intentions. That's understandable. If you do fly off the handle from time to time, it will help if you acknowledge that you hurt your spouse, even though you feel wronged. Your compassion will enhance your partner's ability to be empathetic to you. And that's extremely important. Your partner's empathy is a salient ingredient when it comes to healing. So, be honest and straightforward, but do your best to be kind.

Should discussions be time-limited?

When affairs are first discovered many couples have marathon talk sessions. Some go through the night and for days on end. This is a natural response because when you are in shock, you are trying to make sense of your world. For a while, you might have to do a lot of talking.

But there comes a time when marathon talk sessions become unproductive and hurtful to both of you. This is because *what you focus on expands*. If you are going to limit your attention to the painful aspects of the affair, and nothing else in your life, your days will be saturated with pain. So, there needs to be a balance between talking about what happened and how it has affected you, and other parts of daily living.

In all likelihood, your spouse might be ready to quit the marathon discussions sooner than you are. In fact, he or she may be eager to stop talking about the affair altogether.

I have noticed, with some curiosity, that many couples come to therapy at a specific juncture in their healing process. This junction is typically when the betrayed spouse needs to talk about the affair and the unfaithful spouse wants to stop talking about the affair. The betrayed spouse thinks, "If he isn't willing to help me through this by talking to me about what happened, it means he can't fathom my pain and he's being selfish." Or, "He doesn't love me."

The unfaithful spouse thinks, "I just don't understand how talking about what happened will make things better. We just keep rehashing and rehashing. How in the world can we heal if we keep unburying what is already done?"

As I mentioned earlier, there is truth in both positions: the key is in the balance of the two.

You might consider this third alternative, something I've suggested to many couples that seems to work well. They schedule a predetermined time to have their "affair talks" each week. It might be for an hour, two or three times a week, for example. During those "affair talk times," it is fair and reasonable for you to ask questions and share feelings. Your spouse must agree to sit down with you and hear your feelings and answer your questions. You should set a timer and limit yourself to the time allotted.

When thoughts about the affair come to mind during other parts of the week, rather than discuss them spontaneously, you can remind yourself that you will have time to talk over any lingering issues during the predetermined "talk sessions."

Let me give you an example. I was working with a couple who were at odds about whether or not to keep talking about the affair. Mary, the betrayed spouse, was devastated and needing to talk over lingering feelings. Don, the unfaithful spouse, was growing weary of the difficult conversations and wanted them to come to an end.

I told them that there was value in both of their perspectives and that they had to find a way to both talk about the affair, and at the same time, take a break from it. I gave them the assignment I described above.

On the first night that they had agreed to sit down and discuss the affair, they set the timer for one hour. But when the hour ended, Mary continued to talk about her emotions and other issues. She was aware that her time was up, but she just didn't feel as if she were done. Mary knew that Don had a right to stop her, but he didn't. He allowed her to go on for another half hour without comment.

As it turned out, she so appreciated his flexibility because it signaled to her that he really cared about her feelings that she decided to skip the next bona fide "session." He was thrilled about that and they had a wonderful week together.

Knowing there is a time to talk over questions and thoughts about the betrayal, and a time to focus on other more positive experiences will be helpful to both of you.

Ask for details if it helps

If you're like many people, you might have lots of questions swirling through your mind about what actually happened. You might want to know, "Who was she?" "What does he look like?" "How long has the affair been going on?" "When and where did you meet?" "Did you have feelings for this person?" "Did the children ever meet her?" "What kinds of sexual behaviors did you engage in?" "Was the sex more satisfying with him than it is with me?"

The questions might be endless.

So, what should you do about it? Should you ask for details about the affair, or should you just keep your questions to yourself? Well, it depends. There are advantages and disadvantages when it comes to asking questions.

First, let me say, if you are certain you need information, then ask. Your spouse needs to honor your desire to get a handle on what actually happened. Experience has shown that if one person truly has the need to know what happened, healing won't occur unless the facts are shared.

When the unfaithful spouse is willing to share details, the betrayed spouse often feels as if they are dealing with the problem together openly and honestly. This helps the betrayed spouse make sense of their life. It explains the strange, deceitful behavior and the random absences from home. The dots start to be connected. And although the information may also hurt, many people feel peace in not having to wonder and worry anymore. Better to deal with reality, as tough as it may be to hear, than try to heal the unknown.

Here's what one woman in my practice said about the relief she felt from asking questions:

I feel better about hearing the truth because as horrid as the whole reality was, I don't want to wonder what really went on. I can actually make up worse things than the truth. When I suspected he was cheating, I had imagined he was having sex with *several* women in the neighborhood. And thankfully, that isn't what happened.

For her, the truth paled in comparison to what she'd been dreaming up.

If you're like this woman, go ahead and ask your questions. Know that your questions will probably come in waves. Just when you think that you've thought of everything, a day or two will pass and you will think of another question. This is normal. As I keep saying, this is a process and it will take time.

Although I will address the importance of your spouse being willing to share openly and honestly in Chapter 4, you have a job to do, too. If your spouse is honest with you, as upsetting as it might be to hear the responses, don't attack him or her. Your spouse is doing what you asked- answering your questions. You can say how upset you are with what she or he has done, but always thank him or her for being willing to talk to you about it. You want to encourage rather than punish honesty.

On the other hand, after asking questions, you might not like the answers. Your spouse's responses may hurt you enormously. Plus, once you have information, you might have images in your mind's eye that you didn't have before. You may obsess about the information that was shared. You may regret getting the detailed information that you've been asking about.

When I work with couples, I always ask the betrayed partner, "When you asked those questions and you got the answers, was that helpful?" And if the person says, "Yes, I really feel better now that he is being honest," then I assume it is okay for the betrayed spouse to ask questions.

If, on the other hand, the betrayed partner says, "No, it made me feel really terrible," then asking more questions is not a good idea. I don't recommend it.

So, you should ask yourself the very same questions. After you ask your partner questions, do you feel better or worse? If you feel better, than asking questions will be part of your healing process. If you feel worse, you need to stop asking questions.

Let's say that you fall into the "Need to Stop Asking Questions" camp. I should let you know that, just because you know you feel worse when you've asked questions and received answers; it doesn't mean that you will stop wondering and thinking about lingering loose ends. I can guarantee you that your curiosity will wax and wane. But you have to resist the temptation to ask or you will feel badly. Here's how to avoid the temptation to further question your spouse when you've decided it hurts you more than it helps.

Picture yourself being tempted to ask your mate a question and then ask yourself, "What will I do to resist the temptation? What will I do instead of asking questions?" The "instead" might entail going for walk, taking a hot bath, calling a friend, reading a book, exercising and so on. Just remember that asking questions will be self-sabotaging. Make a list of distractions to take its place that work for you. Then pull out your list whenever you need to refer to it.

One last thought about asking questions. You may have an endless list of questions for another reason, one I haven't yet mentioned. You simply cannot understand how it is possible that your spouse decided to stray. On some level, you are hoping that, by gathering more details or uncovering specific facts, you will be able to make sense of your spouse's choice.

So, you ask and you ask and you ask.

But nothing your spouse says about the logistics of the affair seems to satisfy your gnawing hunger to understand what propelled him or her to make such a seemingly thoughtless choice. You still keep telling yourself, "I would never have done that, how could she have slept with him?" Or, "No matter how unhappy I might be, I never would have chosen to have an affair."

Well, here's the truth. It's entirely possible that you and your spouse *are* different. Your spouse may have deep regrets about the choices that were made, but still, the affair happened. You might be right- you might never, under any circumstances, allow yourself to be unfaithful.

If that's truly the case, no amount of details about the affair will assist you in understanding your spouse's motives for straying. Eventually, it will be helpful for both of you to understand any underlying reasons that the affair occurred. I will help you with this. But knowing more details about where they rendezvoused, what sexual positions they were in, how often they met, and so on, won't help you get a better handle on how your spouse could have allowed him or herself to cheat.

Ask for reassurances without accusing

As you are going through this process, there will be many, many times that you will feel scared, threatened, and insecure about your spouse's actions. You will often wonder whether the affair is over, or if they are sneaking away together, or if they are still contacting each other in any way.

When your spouse is someplace other than in your presence, it is very common for you to wonder and worry about what's really going on. That said, there are a variety of ways to handle these concerns, some clearly better than others. Consider the following example from my practice.

Maggie's husband, Paul, had an affair for two years with his secretary. Eventually, Paul was so guilt-ridden that he disclosed the information to Maggie. Maggie felt as though her world fell apart in that moment. She had suspected that Paul was having an affair, but each time she asked him about it, he denied it. She was crushed that, not only had Paul had an affair, he lied to her about it for so long.

But at last, the truth was out. Paul told Maggie that he ended the affair several weeks earlier and was just waiting for the right time to tell her about it. There never seemed to be a "right" time. Despite Maggie's pain, she wanted to work on their marriage. They both did.

One evening, Maggie got home early from work and decided to make them a nice dinner. Paul said he would be home by 6:00 pm. Maggie was cooking when she noticed that it was 6 o'clock but Paul was not home. She waited for five minutes and then called him on his cell phone, which he did not answer. During the next fifteen minutes, Maggie must have dialed Paul's number six or seven times and still, no answer. By the time Paul walked through the door, twenty-five minutes late, Maggie was in a panic and began to shout.

"Where the hell have you been?" "Were you with her?" "Why aren't you answering my calls?" "I thought you said you had ended the affair. How could you do this to me?"

Paul realized that he'd turned off his cell phone when he was in a business meeting and then forgot to turn it back on. Hence, he missed Maggie's calls. He also failed to notice that he was twenty-five minutes late. In the past, it was common for Paul to return home anywhere between 6 and 6:30 pm. Prior to the disclosure, Maggie had never been upset about the time Paul arrived home.

Although Paul understood why Maggie was upset, he felt

that her questions were incredibly accusatory and her tone, angry. Since Paul had not been with his affair partner, he felt defensive and angry. As a result, instead of answering Maggie's questions and reassuring her- the desired outcome- he retaliated with anger. This, in turn, led to Maggie feeling devastated and suspicious of his real whereabouts.

I spoke to Maggie and told her that it was entirely understandable that she would feel fear, uncertainty, anger and stress because Paul arrived after their agreed upon time. It was equally understandable that her feelings would be heightened when he did not answer his phone. I made it clear that there was no excuse for his forgetting to turn his phone back on or for his failing to realize that he was later than planned.

However, I pointed out that when she accuses him and fires questions at him, she can probably assume that Paul will become defensive and not offer her the support she so desperately wants and needs. I decided to coach Maggie to approach Paul differently if/when the next time she feels out of sorts regarding his whereabouts.

During one of their therapy sessions, I said:

Maggie, rather than automatically accusing Paul of wrongdoing, it would be more helpful if you could say something like the following:

I expected you home by 6 pm. When you were late, I started getting really scared. I started thinking that you were with her again, and that made me feel terrible. The more time that passed, the more scared I became. I started imagining the two of you together somewhere.

It would really help if you told me where you were, and why you were late. It would also help me if you don't turn your phone off. I need to be able to contact you. Plus, if you're going to be later than planned, please call me. Don't make me call you. So, please tell me what happened.

Then I turned to Paul and asked, "If Maggie were to talk to you this way, would this feel different to you,?" and if so, how?" Paul responded,

> That would be great. I would be happy to tell her what happened and that I'm really sorry and it won't happen again. I would also want to comfort her because I know how badly she feels. When she tells me her feelings but doesn't attack me, I want to take care of her.

So, the bottom line is this: when you feel worried, scared and insecure, share your feelings calmly, use the I-messages I referred to before, ask for reassurance rather than attack. Your honesty and vulnerability will make it more likely that your spouse will be loving and caring in return.

Needless to say, there will be times when emotions get the best of you. I understand that. But if your spouse is defensive and angry in response, don't suspect that he or she is hiding something. Accusations tend to lead to counter-attacks, and that's the last thing you need right now. Ask rather than attack.

Identify what has helped and ask for it

In the early stages of dealing with infidelity, you might feel so terrible that you think that nothing is working, that you'll never feel better. But the truth is, there are moments of every day that are just a little better than the rest of the day. There are parts of every week that are better than others. And that's what you need to focus on right now, the tiny reprieves from the pain, the times when you even temporarily "forget" about what has just happened.

I guarantee you that, no matter how bad things are, there are better moments.

So, the first thing you need to do is to ask yourself, "What is different about the times when things aren't quite so bad?" "What's different about the times when I feel a bit of peace?" "What's different about the times when I feel less depressed, angry or anxious?" "What's different about the times when I am coping better than usual?" Keep in mind that it's important not to look for big improvements, tiny baby steps will do.

Let me give you an example.

I recently asked a client of mine, "So, what's different when you feel like you are coping better with the situation?" She answered:

I feel better when we spend time together. My husband has taken some time off from work and that comforts me. When I'm in his presence, I feel better. Just having him there physically makes a difference.

I also feel better when he keeps in touch with me from work. This week he's been calling me three times a day and that feels good.

Another thing. I know he's willing to talk to me about what happened, but this week, he's been asking me how I'm doing without my having to initiate the conversation and that's meant a lot to me.

But there are some things I've been doing for myself that have helped too. I've been exercising nearly every day, even when I feel depressed. I know that's important. I have also been getting together with my closest friend and she has been incredibly supportive. I realize how much I will need my friends to get through this.

After hearing her response, it became clear that there were a number of things she and her husband could do to ease the pain and begin to heal.

If the solutions involved her husband, I suggested that she tell him how helpful his actions have been to her and ask that he continue to do them. There are two parts to this suggestion. First, although she may think that she is entitled to the kindness and concern that she is receiving from her husband, research shows beyond a shadow of a doubt, that the more effective and efficient way to modify behavior (get your spouse to act in a certain way), is positive reinforcement.

She needs to observe what he does that is working, even a little, and acknowledge his efforts. This encouragement will go a long way towards helping him want to please her. She does deserve kindness and concern, and he deserves acknowledgement. They're both important to the process of healing.

Secondly, once she is aware of what her husband does that is helpful, she needs to point out these things- his actions or words- and let him know exactly what's working to comfort her. She should not expect her husband to figure it out on his own. She needs to coach him and be specific about her wants and needs.

Expect major ups and downs

I can't tell you this often enough; the road to recovery is paved with many, many ups and downs. Just when you think you're feeling better, something will happen that will send you spiraling downward and once again, you'll wonder if things will ever improve. In fact, you will be doubtful real change can happen.

This simply isn't true. Your bad feelings will come in waves. They will be interspersed with calmer moments. During the calm moments, you will feel hopeful. When something occurs that triggers you, and sends you emotionally spiraling, you may doubt yourself, your spouse and whether it's even worth continuing to work on your marriage. This is completely normal, and you need to expect these times will come. But expecting that tough times will come isn't enough: you need to have a plan in place to prepare for them, and to keep you from overreacting.

Find ways to get back on track

As I've said, setbacks are normal. In fact, each setback gives you and your spouse an opportunity to learn ways to get back on track. What separates the winners from the losers when it comes to healing from infidelity is not whether or not you have relapses- because you will- but how quickly and efficiently you get yourselves back on track.

One of the things that slows progress for getting back on track after a bad day or week is judgmental thoughts about the slip. You might think, "I can't believe we're back at this place again," or "See, I knew things weren't going to last," or "I can't take these ups and downs anymore," or "Going backwards makes me feel so badly." Although these thoughts are normal, please don't give them much weight. That's because if you do, you will worry about the relapse *and* you will also feel hopeless.

Instead, it helps to just tell yourself, "Michele said relapses are normal. This is how it's going to be for a while. We'll get through this. Tomorrow will be better." In other words, you have to find ways to self-soothe. Staying centered will help you do what you need to do to move forward again.

So, when you hit a bump in the road, ask yourself, "What do I need to do to get things back on track," or "What did I/my spouse do that was helpful the last time that we had a relapse?" Develop a list of strategies that you've used to move past the bad feelings, drawing on what has worked in the past.

For example, think about how you and your spouse made up or reconciled after a drop in spirits. Did you approach your spouse or did he or she approach you? What did either of you do that made things better? Did you talk about what happened? Did you just let time pass? Once you identify what helped, you just have to consciously implement that plan again. A simple but profound tenet of my therapy practice is to have couples notice what works and encourage them to do more of that. The converse is also true: notice what doesn't work, and do less of that. It's a simple way of living life that produces profoundly positive results.

And another thing about setbacks; like snowflakes, no two are exactly alike. It helps to figure out how the current setback differs from the one before. For instance, although you had an argument with your spouse, was it less intense than arguments in the past? Did you get yourselves back on track more quickly? Ask yourself, "How is this setback different from the one we had last week/month?" It helps to see improvements even when you have taken a step backwards. You will feel less discouraged when you can see forward motion.

Taking care of yourself

Although I truly believe that your spouse has to help you through this process, it doesn't dismiss the fact that you need to do some self-healing; you have to take good care of yourself. The affair has probably left you feeling a multitude of emotions- depressed, anxious, questioning your sex appeal, insecure, worried about the future, resentment, anger and so on. In addition to the comfort your spouse can offer you, you need to find ways to help yourself to feel better.

Prior to the infidelity, you had coping mechanisms that helped you right yourself when you have had bad days. Try to recall what you have done in the past that helped you stay centered. Here's a list of what has worked for some people in your shoes:

- Exercise / Yoga

- Meditation

- Prayer or attending church/synagogue

- Being with friends or relatives

- Playing an instrument

- Reading books that are inspirational

- Going for therapy

- Taking a trip

- Staying focused on work or hobbies

- Being present with your children

- Spending time in nature

- Keeping a journal

Everyone's list is different. But it is important that you create your own unique list. Then, no matter how you're feeling, force yourself to do at least one thing every day that makes you feel accomplished. I know this can be challenging, especially in the beginning, but I also know that it is absolutely necessary. You need something in your life to feed your soul.

You see, like I said before, even though your spouse has a responsibility to be helpful to you, in the end, you have to also rely on yourself. You have to self-soothe. When you do, you will feel empowered and this will help you move forward.

You have to remember that your partner's decision to stray doesn't lessen you as a person. I worked with a woman who told me that, though she had worked through her many self-esteem problems growing up, she began questioning her self-worth all over again when she found out that her husband had an affair.

I reminded her that her husband's decision to have an affair didn't change who she was as a person. Although her husband felt something missing in their relationship, no one forced him to have an affair because of it. His choice to go outside of his marriage rather than work on the issues between them said something about his problem-solving skills, not a deficit in her. I assured her that she was no less lovable because her husband strayed. She needed to spend time rebuilding the positive feelings she had about herself before the revelations that upended her world.

She also told me that she feels "less than" courageous because she chose to stay with a person who betrayed her. In fact, she carried some shame about her decision to stay rather than walk away.

This is not uncommon. Many of the people I work with tell me, "I feel bad about myself that I'm staying married to him or her. I should have more self-esteem. I should have the courage to leave. There must be something wrong with me that I'm willing to put up with this."

Hear this. There is no shame in staying. In fact, most people do, and for those who do, it is quite the opposite of shame: it takes an incredible amount of courage to stay and work on a relationship in the face of such hurt. Infidelity is more common than most realize and the truth is that most marriages survive it. When you decide to stay after you've been betrayed, you do it for *your* reasons, for the things you value in life such as commitment, family and a shared history. You are trying to learn from life's experiences and grow despite the pain.

This is the sign of a strong, brave person, not someone deserving of shame. You should feel proud of your desire and dedication to working through hard times. That's what life's about. Feel good about yourself for your willingness to stay.

If you feel that you need additional support to love yourself again after you have felt discombobulated, you should definitely consider getting some professional help for yourself.

Make sure that you go to a therapist who believes in the sanctity of marriage, who doesn't assume that infidelity is a marital deal breaker. Put a great deal of effort into finding a therapist who will support both you and your marriage. I wrote a helpful article about choosing a marital therapist and you can read it on my website. Also, later in the book, I will give you some information about additional resources for you and your spouse including Divorce Busting® Telephone Coaching and personal 2-day sessions with me.

Though the feelings you're having right now have been triggered by the current crisis of infidelity, you have to find effective ways to soothe yourself. Learning to self-soothe is a skill that will serve you all your life, in any number of painful or traumatic situations. (One "plus" of surviving an affair is that after you make it through this, you'll know that you have the inner strength and resources to survive almost anything life throws at you!) You can do it.

The next chapter is for your spouse. Of course, you can and should read it too. It will help you both be on the same page during this process. There is more work for you to do too. I outline your next steps in Chapter 5. So, work on the tasks described in this chapter and then I'll "coach" you again soon.

CHAPTER FOUR
THE UNFAITHFUL
SPOUSE'S TASKS

I N THE LAST chapter, I coached your spouse to do things that would help him or her feel better. Much of what I suggested will help you too because your interactions will be less hurtful and more productive. I know this will be a relief to you because, if you're like other people surviving the aftermath of an affair, it's not just your spouse who has been hurting; you have also been reeling since the discovery of the affair. The discovery marks a turning point in your life.

And speaking of the discovery, it may have happened in a variety of ways. Your spouse might have been snooping and uncovered questionable phone bills, hotel receipts, suggestive texts, photos or other incriminating evidence and then confronted you with it. Perhaps you initially covered your tracks and lied about your actions in the past. Or perhaps a friend or acquaintance found out about the affair, or saw you with the affair partner in a more-than-friend embrace, and told your spouse. Perhaps an affair was discovered at work, and one of you was asked to leave the workplace. But the fact that you're reading this now tells me that you have come clean. And that's a good thing. Now the cards are on the table and you can begin to forge forward and start the healing process.

Perhaps your spouse didn't discover the affair. You might have volunteered the information because living a lie has been too overwhelming for you. After years of working with couples where infidelity has been an issue, I can tell you one thing for sure: no matter how much pleasure people derive from their affairs, there are almost always tremendous feelings of guilt, shame and duplicitousness. You constantly feel torn. This is best described in a wonderful article by Wendy Plump entitled, *A Roomful of Yearning and Regret*. She writes, "This (having an affair) is no way for an adult to live. When you're with your lover, you'll be working on your alibi and feeling loathsome. When you're with your spouse, you'll be dying to return to your love nest." This tug-of-war can be crazy-making.

But now, the truth is out. You have stepped into the light. You don't have to lie any longer. And because this is so, you might be taking a deep sigh of relief. Some people tell me that it's the best they have felt in a long time.

What you have to keep in mind, however, is that you and your spouse are not on parallel paths right now. You may feel as though a door has opened and you can see the light; your spouse, however, may be feeling imprisoned. You're feeling lighter just as your spouse is starting the darkest time of his or her life. This is one of the dilemmas that makes the process so challenging.

That's why I'm here. Even though you and your spouse might be in very different places right now, I am going to tell you what you need to do to rebuild trust, feel better about yourself and each other, and strengthen your marriage.

In the early stages of recovery, you have a lot of work to do. In fact, you may feel that the lion's share of work to heal rests on your shoulders. I won't disagree with that. You have to restore your spouse's faith in you as a marital partner. That will take work. That will take time. But I will lead the way.

Before I begin coaching you, I want you to know that later in the process, we will take a look at the reasons you chose to have an affair. You may feel that a gaping hole in your marriage is what led you to stray. You might believe that if your marriage had been more fulfilling, this wouldn't have happened.

Your marriage might be in need of a major overhaul and we will definitely address that later- I promise- but for now, you have to accept personal responsibility for your actions. So, here is a list of actions you need to take to begin to reconnect with your spouse.

End the affair

I have worked with countless people over the years who want to reconcile with their spouses after an affair. Some have given up their affair partner, others haven't. It is my experience that it is almost impossible to truly put energy and effort into your marriage if you continue to see your affair partner. Your emotional energy is finite. And you'll need all of it to go in just one direction: toward healing your marriage. Ending the affair marks the beginning of working on your marriage in earnest.

But endings don't always happen quickly. Sometimes, especially if the affair has been on-going for a long time, people break away from their affair partners gradually. Even if people's intentions are good- they truly want to end the affairs- things can be complicated. Often, affair partners resist ending the relationship, escalating their behavior, hoping to stay engaged with you, to maintain the status quo.

Whether you have decided to quit cold turkey, or you are breaking away gradually, the bottom line is that you must eventually end the affair if you sincerely want your marriage to work. And how you end the affair makes a difference.

Although in a 1975 hit song by Simon and Garfunkel we were told that there are "50 Ways to Leave Your Lover," in truth there is only one. Endings have to be definitive and final. They have to be black and white. Any gray area will be misinterpreted. Let me give you an example.

I was working with a man who wanted to end his affair. When I heard a bit about the nature of the relationship, I predicted that it wasn't going to be easy. The affair partner, a woman, was convinced that my client was going to leave his wife. From what I'd heard from him, I sensed that she was not going to let go of the relationship easily.

When I asked the husband to tell me what he actually told his affair partner, he said, "I told her, 'I love you and I always will, but I am going to try to work on my marriage right now. I need to stop seeing you.' " Let's pause here to examine what is wrong with this statement.

Because he started off with telling the affair partner that he loved her and "always would," she could easily focus on his undying feelings for her and disregard whatever he said next. Plus, his comment, "I'm going to *try* to work on my marriage *right now*," made a clear-cut breakup even less likely for two reasons.

Note that he said, "…but I am going to *try* to work on my marriage." My mother, a therapist, used to say, "There are those who *try* and those who *do*." I agree wholeheartedly. "Trying" connotes tentativeness, when what is needed is absolute clarity and decisiveness. Secondly, when he says that he is "…going to try to work on his marriage *right now*," he's leaving himself an out.

It sounds like he is going to work on his marriage and see what happens. And that this is likely a temporary effort. Any affair partner who wants to sustain the relationship would be justified in feeling hopeful. It's easy to read between the lines and believe that the affair still has potential.

Ending an affair also means cutting off communication: no calls, no texts, no IM's, nothing. This is challenging to do when their affair partner continues to correspond. It's easy to think, "I can't be rude and not respond," or "I'll just check in *as a friend* to see how she's doing," or "I'll just ask her not to text me anymore." But any response is a way of saying, "I am still in contact with you." As hard as it is, if you are serious about repairing your marriage, it is kinder to the affair partner to make a clean, clear, concise break. Ending means ending.

It's important to realize that it's entirely possible that, no matter how you end the affair, your affair partner will still try to escalate his or her efforts to connect with you. The more you pull away, the more your affair partner will pursue you. You need to be strong and remember why you are doing what you are doing: you want your marriage back.

Chances are, if the affair held any meaning for you at all, it will be very hard to pull away, even if your intentions to work on your marriage are sound. There are several reasons that letting go of the relationship might be challenging. It's possible that many of your emotional needs were being met by that relationship. It's hard to imagine those needs suddenly going unmet, especially if your marriage was less than it should have been.

Another reason that "breaking up is hard to do," even if you're done with the relationship, is that you might feel guilty about hurting your affair partner who doesn't share your sentiment about ending things. Perhaps you just want the affair to go away, but you don't want to hurt anyone. Let me say with all the honesty and compassion I can: it is impossible not to hurt him or her if they still have feelings for you. You can tell your affair partner that you are very regretful about hurting him or her. That said, if you truly want to minimize their hurt, be clear about your intentions. Don't put off the inevitable. Don't prolong the hurt. Just make a clean break.

One final word about breaking up. Many people ask whether or not they should see their affair partner in person to end the relationship. Although everyone is different, being face-to-face creates temptations that won't occur if the break up happens over the phone or through email. It may seem cold, but in the long run, it might be the kindest way to dissolve the affair. Once the affair has ended, you can put your heart into working on your marriage.

If your affair partner continues to try to contact you, then you will want to take the following steps:

- Continue to ignore contact from the affair partner. Any response on your part can be viewed as a sign of hope that you are re-engaging. Be patient if your affair partner is persistent. It may take a while for them to recognize that you are serious about ending the relationship.

- Inform your spouse when you receive contact of any kind so you can decide how to respond as a team.

- Block your affair partner's phone number and email address so you won't feel tempted to connect if he or she calls, texts or emails.

- If you accidentally run into your affair partner, politely say hello, but do not enter into a conversation.

Spend time together

As I said in Chapter 2, most betrayed people tell me that it really helps when they spend time with their spouses after the discovery of infidelity. Being together feels safe. It's when the unfaithful spouse is out of sight that things become considerably more tenuous. There are suspicions and fears. There is anxiety. Negative thoughts and rumination are the rule.

So, whatever you can do to spend time with your spouse right now during this crisis period is extremely important. If you have flexibility at work, take time off. Make yourself available to be present, to talk, or to do whatever your spouse needs you to do right now. Since their life is focused solely on adjusting to the truth of the affair right now, they may feel resentful that your life simply goes on "normally." Even though you might be feeling terrible too, when you're apart from each other, your spouse may perceive that you are unfazed by what has happened. When you're together, your spouse can see the impact this ordeal is having on you.

So, be around. Be present. Be loving.

If you can't take time off of work or the responsibilities you have during the day, you should make a concerted effort to stay in touch with your spouse and asking him or her how things are going. Show an interest in your spouse's well-being. Call, send texts or email several times throughout the day. The contact will show that you care.

Share details

Although this varies from person to person, many people who have been betrayed have lots of questions about the affair, especially early on in the process. In the last chapter, directed to your spouse,

I mentioned sometimes the questions and conversations about "what happened" go on until the wee hours of morn, day after day.

To you, it might seem that there is no end to the questions. You can't understand how rehashing the past will fix anything. You wonder how you should respond to questions when you know that the answers will be hurtful to your spouse. Should you tell the truth? Should you minimize what happened? Should you avoid answering altogether?

Here's my advice. I have coached your spouse about whether or not to ask questions regarding the affair. Some people find it incredibly helpful to get the whole truth, while others are hurt by the information. It is your spouse's responsibility to determine which category he or she fits into. Not yours. If your spouse has questions, you need to be willing to answer them completely and honestly. Yes, even if it sends him or her reeling backwards for a bit.

Because you have betrayed your spouse, it is essential that, in moving forward, you make every effort to be as open and honest as possible. This will be the only way that your spouse will want to trust you again. When you share the details of what happened, especially the dynamics of how one thing led to another, your spouse may suddenly feel that you are on the same team again, working at getting through this together. One of the most hurtful parts about infidelity is the secrets that you have shared with another person. Coming clean with your partner about your actions places the two of you side by side again. This is both reassuring and reinforcing.

On the other hand, it is entirely possible that he or she will become enraged, hurt, critical and even abusive when you share detailed answers to their questions. It's your job to stay calm and try not to be reactive. Just let your spouse know that you completely understand why he or she is angry, hurt, or ___ (fill in the blank.) You realize that you have done something that has truly broken his or her heart and you can understand the reaction. Even if you feel defensive, don't defend yourself. Don't attack. Just say you're sorry.

I'll be saying more about apologies shortly; but in the meantime, just know that when your spouse gets angry, the deeper emotion beneath that anger is really *hurt*. You can soften the hurt by showing your concern rather than defending yourself. I know this is asking a lot of you, but you've got to practice staying calm and being there emotionally for your spouse. Take deep breaths. It will help.

Here's another common happening: you might have the urge to withhold information or tell a little white lie to avoid the repercussions of telling the truth or hurting your partner. Don't do it! Here's why.

I've worked with many couples and trust me on this: when the betrayed spouse discovers their husband or wife has not been completely forthcoming, things get worse, and fast. You do not want your mate to find out additional or conflicting information about the affair weeks or months after the discovery. No matter how well things were going in your marriage at the time, things will likely go downhill drastically.

Leaking information a little at a time can be a marital death sentence. If you are withholding information, and it comes out in small bits and pieces down the road, it re-traumatizes your spouse. Don't let that happen. Be completely forthcoming at once. It will be difficult, but not nearly as difficult as having to tell your partner that you weren't telling the whole truth in the beginning. Lies are damaging, especially when you're in the process of rebuilding trust.

Your being honest about what happened is important for another reason. Your spouse's life has been turned upside down. He or she might have suspected that you were unfaithful and you probably lied, dodged or demurred whenever possible. That's when your spouse began to mistrust his or her own instincts. He or she might have thought, "I'm imagining things," or "I'm paranoid," or, "I'm making a mountain out of a molehill." Not wanting to get caught, you might have encouraged your spouse to doubt their own intuition.

Now that the truth is out, your spouse is trying to make sense of his or her life, to connect the dots and wrap his or her brain around what really happened. You need to help your spouse do that, no matter how difficult that might be for you.

For some people, it's incredibly difficult to talk about the affair because it makes them feel ashamed. Shame is a very powerful emotion. It's one thing to think that you've *done* something bad. That's called guilt. But shame runs deeper than that. People who feel shame believe that *they're* bad people. And that can feel debilitating.

If you are feeling shame right now, consider this. As hard as it might be for you to be experiencing this dark emotion, you need to know that it means you have a conscience and that you have integrity. You never meant to hurt your spouse. It crushes you to see him or her suffering. So, talking about your failure to be faithful only makes you feel worse.

If shame is preventing you from talking to your spouse about the affair, you can't let that happen. You need to remind yourself that you are not a bad person because you decided to stray. You might have made a decision that was not in your marriage's best interest; but you probably are a kind, loving person or you wouldn't be reading this and wanting to set your marriage back on course.

As long as you are focusing on shame or the guilt you feel in hurting your spouse, you won't be available emotionally; you are too wrapped up into yourself. The best way to work through the guilt and shame is to make a commitment to help your spouse heal through loving, kind acts initiated by you. Really be there. Be accountable. Don't go inward. Don't escape into your own pain. Stay present with your partner. Show your concern.

If your shame has got a grip on you, you might consider getting some additional individual help to dig out from the emotional hole. Sometimes the hardest person to forgive in this life is yourself. This is where a compassionate counselor can help you talk about your own issues and move on to forgiving yourself, so that you can be available to your spouse.

I was working with a couple who had dealt with the pain of betrayal for many years. The husband had been involved in two affairs, one of which resulted in a child with the affair partner. He was so ashamed of his behavior that he rarely spoke about what happened and never truly apologized to his wife. She suffered for years.

During my session with them, it was clear that he was incredibly uncomfortable talking about what had happened and about the void between the two of them due to his unwillingness to address the pain directly.

When I asked him whether he was sorry about what happened, he said, "Of course, otherwise I wouldn't be here now. I wouldn't have worked so hard to support my family all these years if she weren't important to me." This was hardly a heart-felt, genuine apology. When I confronted him about that, he started to talk about his deep shame and guilt for the first time in their marriage.

He cried as he talked about hating himself for what he had done. He told his wife that he knew she suffered all these years because of the choices he made. He admitted that he always thought she deserved someone better than him in her life. He felt that saying, "I'm sorry," just wasn't enough; but he didn't know what else to do. Because he felt such despair inside, he just kept his distance.

I reassured him that, from what I could tell, he was a kind person who cared deeply about his children and extended family. He was a good provider and wanted more than anything for things to be better between him and his wife. I encouraged him to stop berating himself, to look at his wife and tell her what she obviously needed to hear from him.

For the first time in the history of their marriage, he apologized wholeheartedly. He cried. He asked for forgiveness. And much to his surprise, his wife who had been waiting for years to see some empathy and vulnerability, was extremely receptive to hearing his remorse. By focusing on her and her pain as opposed to his feelings of shame, they were beginning to heal....together.

One final thought about discussing the affair. Countless betrayed spouses have told me they resent being the ones who always seem to bring up the affair and its impact on the marriage. If you want to help your spouse feel better, even if you're not up for it, ask him or her, "How are you doing today?" "What's on your mind?" "Is there anything you'd like to talk to me about right now?" When *you* initiate the conversation, it shows that you really care.

Show remorse

Here's the truth. Your spouse is really hurting right now. And he or she sees you and your actions as the source of the pain. Although you can't undo the past, you can do something proactive in the present that will help mitigate the pain.

Time and time again, betrayed people have told me that one of the most important actions that their partners can take to help them heal from infidelity is to demonstrate that they are truly sorry for the hurt they have caused. Even if you don't completely regret your choice to have had an affair because it fulfilled some unmet needs in your life, or it helped you feel alive again, I'm certain you never meant to hurt your spouse.

But the end result is that your spouse is really struggling right now and that's what you need to focus on: things you can do to ease their pain. But how?

Of course, you'll want to show remorse through your actions, through your dedication to working through this tough transitional period. When you follow the suggestions in this book, taking actions you should take and really sticking with the program, your spouse will see you as taking personal responsibility for improving your marriage and caring about his or her feelings. As the saying goes, "Actions speak louder than words." And although that's completely true, most betrayed spouses need to hear words of apology as well.

Start by saying, "I'm sorry." But saying I'm sorry isn't enough. You have to go into details about *why* you're sorry. You have to explain your understanding about how your actions have impacted on your spouse. You need to try to put yourself into your spouse's shoes and imagine how it might feel if the tables were turned. Don't hurry through your apology. Be thorough. List all the reasons your decision to stray created emotional stress for your spouse.

Here's something else you should know about apologies. They have to be sincere. Your spouse now has radar for anything that feels less than genuine. Wait until the right moment, when you're feeling a real desire to express your sadness about what's transpired, and sit your partner down to share your feelings. Make sure the words aren't empty. *Show* your emotions. Countless people have told me that they didn't feel that their partners' apologies were real because when their partners expressed regret, their affect (facial expression) didn't change. They didn't cry, they didn't even look sad. So, don't fight back the tears, if you feel them. Show your spouse what's inside of you. Showing your emotions helps your partner know that you truly care about their feelings.

Look them in the eye if you can, so they can see the depth of your emotions. Eyes are the windows to the soul. And it is likely that you looked or glanced away quite a bit when you were being actively unfaithful. Your M.O. was to avoid. Now your M.O. must be to connect.

And one more important point. When I suggest that people apologize to their spouses, they often tell me, "I already did," or "I have, several times." Here's what you need to know about saying I'm sorry. You have to do it often. In fact, you may have to apologize periodically for a long time to come. That's because your spouse's pain comes in waves. Don't keep score of the number of times you expressed remorse. Just know that every time you do, you are helping your spouse feel a little bit better.

Sometimes, if your words do not seem to carry enough weight, you might consider writing a letter or sending a card of apology as well. In fact, it might take more than one. If, in the past, letter writing or card-giving has pleased your spouse, it could once again be an effective means of touching your spouse's heart right now.

Finally, if your spouse keeps saying, "You don't seem contrite, remorseful or sorry," ask them, "What would I have to do, specifically, to help you see that I am truly sorry?" Try to get your spouse to talk about specific actions you should take to show your remorse. Everyone has slightly different expectations about what it means to be sorry. Find out your spouse's definition and then do it.

Here are a couple of examples. A betrayed spouse might say, "If you are really sorry, you will want me to be happier in this marriage. You've never shown an interest in my parents. I'd like for you to be willing to go out to dinner with them once in a while." Or, "If you are really sorry, you'd be willing to end your affair on the phone, rather than seeing her face-to-face. Plus, you'd let me be in the room when you call her." Or, "I will know you are sorry about what you did when you show me that you value me as a person. You can do this by supporting me more with our kids. Just because I'm a stay-at-home mom, doesn't mean you can abdicate all responsibilities when you get home." Whatever your spouse indicates is a sign of remorse is what you should be doing.

Demonstrate real empathy

Betrayed spouses often say, "My husband just doesn't get it." Or, "My wife has absolutely no idea what I'm going through." In order to heal, it helps to feel that you are making an effort to understand what your spouse is feeling. This isn't about remorse as much as it is about empathy. It's not about saying, "I'm sorry." It's about letting your spouse know that you can understand why he or she is so_____ (angry, hurt, devastated, or confused).

When your spouse is discussing how she or he feels, it helps for you to simply say, "I get it. I can understand why you would feel this way. If I were in your position, I would struggle to trust as well." And then explain why those feelings make sense to you. Don't debate. Don't tell your spouse that she or he is over-reacting or that she or he shouldn't feel a particular way. For example, if, as a result of your affair, your wife questions whether you ever loved her at all, don't tell her that she's over-reacting. If it is in fact true, you can reassure her that you do love her, but add that you can understand why she might be questioning your love at this time. In other words, it's important to validate feelings.

If your spouse continues to say that you aren't being empathetic, or that you don't care about his or her feelings, it is useful to ask where you're missing the mark. Ask the question, "If I were more empathetic, if I really got it, what would I do that I haven't been doing?" And again, help your spouse be specific about actions you can take that might make a difference.

For example, a wife told her husband that she would know that he was being empathetic if he was willing to talk about her feelings more often. She also wanted him to repeat back his understanding of what she said, to insure that he "got it." She told him, "You don't even have to agree with everything I'm saying. I just want to make sure you're listening, and comprehend how I feel."

The truth is, unless you have been in the same situation and felt as badly about it as your spouse, you probably won't be able to understand what it's like for your spouse to be going through this "season of emotional suffering." In fact, you might tell your spouse, "I can't possibly completely understand your pain, but I want to do whatever I can to help you through it."

As I have said several times, one of the tough issues about the healing process is that you and your spouse are probably at very different junctures right now. You have put your cards on the table and, in all likelihood, are feeling some relief. In fact, you might feel tremendous relief. Your spouse, on the other hand, is probably in a very, very dark place. Since you can't enter into your spouse's reality, the best you can do is to validate feelings and show that you sincerely care.

Your spouse might test you to see if you are going to remain dedicated to the mission of saving your marriage by saying hurtful things to you. This is your chance to prove your commitment to work things out. If your spouse verbally attacks you, take a deep breath. Say, "I know you're hurting, I'm happy to _____ (answer your questions, explain why I did what I did, talk to you about this, and so on) but please don't attack me. We'll get a lot further if we're kind to each other."

Expect ups and downs

Are you a Type-A personality? Are you used to setting a goal, pushing up your sleeves and making it happen? Well, guess what. This time you simply can't plow through a formula and get a quick result. The healing process takes time. And furthermore, there are lots and lots of ups and downs. Here's an example of what you can expect.

The affair gets discovered. At first, all hell breaks loose. Then there are talks, explanations, revelations and more disclosures. After a while, progress appears to be made. You even have times when you're not talking about the affair. There are glimmers of hope that this awful period won't last for the rest of your life.

But then something reminds your spouse of the affair. You end up fighting for the rest of the week. You wonder if the bad times are ever going to end.

A few days later, the ice melts; you're on speaking terms again. Finally. So, you start thinking everything is going to be okay again. And, for a while, it is. Sure, you have your talks and questioning periods, but they seem to end on relatively decent notes. You're hopeful again.

But not long after that, your spouse has bad dreams about you having an affair and he or she is furious. Again, there are angry words, cold shoulders and nasty daily interactions. You begin to think things will never change.

Get the picture? It's up and down and up and down. And I know how discouraging this can be, particularly if you are trying hard to be a good person and partner. But I've never met a couple who didn't experience this roller coaster ride. That's why I warned you early on to fasten your seat belt because you're in for a bumpy ride.

When you hit a low, you will eventually ask yourself whether all this pain is worth it. You might question whether you and your spouse are meant to be together after all. That's understandable. But here's what I've learned from decades of specializing in working with couples who've experienced betrayal.

As long as you don't over-react when you hit the bumps in the road, you'll be fine. When it seems like all the progress you've been making has gone right out the window, remind yourself that real change, the kind that sticks, is three steps forward and two steps back. That's true for anyone trying to make fundamental changes in life, not just when overcoming infidelity.

And when the two of you take two steps back, it is easy to feel as though you've lost all momentum, but that's simply not the case. Change is a process. It's a zig-zag rather than a straight line. Remember: as long as the trajectory is going in the upward direction, all is well. You are moving forward gradually. And that's how recovery happens....gradually.

Because recovery happens gradually, it means you have to be patient. Having unreasonable expectations about how quickly you will feel totally happy and at ease in your own marriage again, is sure to make you miserable. You'll get angry. You'll pull away. And both of those actions will impede progress in a big way. Just tell yourself that this will take time, but your marriage and your family are worth the wait.

Be willing to do what it takes to reassure your partner

Okay. Here's where the rubber meets the road. Your spouse is feeling insecure, suspicious and scared. And it's your job to do whatever you can to rebuild lost trust. That means that you are going to have to honor your spouse's requests to do a number of things that you ordinarily wouldn't do. Your life needs to be an open book. Let me explain.

You need to be willing to do whatever your spouse asks you to do that will make him or her feel reassured. That might include, but won't be limited to, sharing passwords to email and Facebook accounts, along with telephone or credit card bills. It might also include offering access to text messages and other personal items on your phone. Your spouse might want to see bank statements. You should demonstrate your willingness to share information freely and openly.

Additionally, your spouse might become anxious when you aren't in each other's presence and want to know specifics regarding your whereabouts. In that case, you need to offer detailed information about your day, your itinerary and the people you'll encounter along the way. Be honest and concrete.

Your spouse might want you to contact him or her throughout the day, just to check in. Some people ask their unfaithful spouses to call from a landline to verify their location. Clearly, not everyone has access to a landline, but if that's the request, honor it, if possible. If your spouse asks you to check in throughout the day; then by all means, call, text and email just to say hi and ask how their day is going.

If you travel out of town for work, your spouse may request to go along with you, or that you limit your travel. It's important that you make this adjustment for now, whenever possible. Similarly, if your affair partner is a co-worker or employee and your spouse asks you to move to another department or get a different job, the request should be seriously considered. It is not always possible to make such a change when it comes to employment, but whatever can be done to create an environment that doesn't constantly trigger pain for your spouse is important.

If the affair partner lives in your neighborhood (and particularly if any of your rendezvous occurred in your own home), it is not too drastic to consider moving. A hassle, yes. But always weigh geographical and work changes to the dramatic and long-lasting upheaval of going through a divorce and dividing up your family for a lifetime. Divorce is incredibly costly. Use whatever funds you can afford, and make whatever schedule changes you can, so that your lifestyle becomes more marriage-friendly.

If the affair partner was a work-place colleague and it isn't possible for you to shift positions or jobs, it is going to be much tougher for your spouse to feel reassured. You will have to discuss what you can do that will comfort your betrayed spouse. Otherwise, anxiety will be overwhelming and progress may spiral downward. If changing work environments isn't realistic, ask your spouse, "What can I do other than ____(quit my job, fire my employee, change departments) that will help you feel better when I go to work each day?" Ask, "What can I do to help you feel reassured?"

For example, one husband, whose wife had an affair, said that he would really like to show up at her workplace from time to time so that they could go out to lunch together. He also asked that his wife tell her affair partner that she was not going to work on projects with him anymore. Finally, he requested that his wife cut back on the long hours she usually spent at work and come home earlier. She agreed to all of these actions.

Perhaps, as you've been reading this, you are thinking to yourself, "I feel like I'm a child and my spouse is my parent." Or, "This feels like incarceration. I don't want to be in jail in my marriage." Those feelings are completely understandable. The previous suggestions are no way to live. No one wants to live under this sort of scrutiny as a permanent way of life.

That said, I am not suggesting that you do these things forever.

You see, you are in the throes of a crisis period. And sometimes, when you are muddling through a crisis, you have to agree to accommodate your traumatized partner in ways you might not ordinarily agree to do. During this time period, your partner needs extra care and lots of reassurances. Try to remember that you both are in a transitional period. You won't have to report in, or feel under a microscope forever. There will be a beginning, middle and end to this time.

For the time being, you are working at winning back your spouse's trust and faith in you. Your spouse feels deeply betrayed and you need to make amends. Your willingness to do whatever it takes- come clean and be reassuring- will show your spouse that you are loyal and trustworthy. This will go a long way to helping you both recover. For now, you owe your spouse this sort of transparency.

Examine personal reasons the affair occurred

One of the things you will need to do both for yourself and your spouse is to give some thought to why you decided to have an affair. Many a betrayed spouse has shared, "I won't feel safe until I have a better understanding about why my husband strayed." Or, "Until I know how and why my wife could be unfaithful to me, I'll remain afraid it can happen again."

Perhaps you think that you didn't mean to have an affair, it just happened. Here's what I think about that.

Affairs aren't spontaneous; they require careful planning and decision-making. Often, the choices people make, one step after another, pave the way for an affair: dinner with a co-worker; meeting an old boyfriend or girlfriend for a drink after work just to catch up; having lunch with an attractive, single neighbor on a regular basis; connecting with an old flame via social media; or sending a lengthy Christmas update to a long lost heart throb can all seem relatively innocent.

But one dinner date or late night conversation often leads to another and another and another. The talk becomes more personal. Confessions of marital dissatisfaction bubble to the surface prompting empathy and support. People tell themselves, "I just needed someone to talk to. I wanted input from someone of the opposite sex."

But you don't need a degree in psychology to know that the implicit message in these conversations is, "I'm unhappily married. Want to fool around?" You can tell yourself that you're not doing anything wrong, but the truth is, it's a sheer, slippery slope.

What about people who feel stuck in truly bad marriages? Doesn't such unhappiness justify being unfaithful? After all, life is short. We only have one go around, right?

What's always amazed me is how differently people react to similar circumstances. I've met people whose spouses refused to have sex with them for years and although this neglect left them lonely and miserable, they simply could not cheat on their mate. I've met other people who, when their relationships hit predictable bumps in the road, sought comfort in the arms of strangers rather than work things out. Unhappy marriages don't *cause* infidelity. Being unfaithful causes infidelity.

I have compassion for those who truly feel lonely in their marriage; this is no way to live. But dulling relational pain through the instant gratification of hot sex or emotional closeness with someone who doesn't argue with you about bills, children or the in-laws isn't an effective or lasting way to fix what's wrong. In fact, infidelity complicates life enormously for everyone involved. I assume you know this by now and you're looking for solutions to make life better all around.

So, let's take a look at some reasons people choose to go outside their marriages to fulfill they're needs.

- **In search of better sex**

Some people seek new sexual partners because they are unhappy with their sexual relationships. They may feel that sex has become routine, boring or passionless. Sometimes there isn't enough sex or a marriage has turned sexless. When this happens, the partner whose sexual needs and desires go unmet can feel an extreme sense of rejection and unhappiness. Many people decide that they're not going to live their lives in a sex-lite or passionless marriage and feel compelled to do something about it. They desperately want to feel wanted.

By the way, if this sounds like you, I would strongly suggest that you read my book, THE SEX-STARVED MARRIAGE, or watch my TEDx talk by the same title. It will help you feel validated and offer some suggestions for both of you.

- **Emotional needs aren't being satisfied in marriage**

Many people tell me they had an affair because they felt lonely in their marriages. There was an emotional disconnect. They may feel like roommates but not lovers.

There are lots of reasons couples stop feeling close and connected in relationships. Sometimes they haven't been spending enough time together as a couple. They haven't been nurturing their marriages. Other times they have a hard time talking about intimate and important subjects. They often have trouble resolving challenging problems; sticky issues either get swept under the carpet or argued about. When this happens, people often say things like, "I've fallen out of love with my husband." Or, "I don't feel any emotional connection or intimacy with my wife anymore."

If you feel that you've fallen out of love with your spouse, it makes infidelity very compelling. Why? Because when you're with your affair partner, you feel alive and filled with passion. Affair partners are often very flattering, attentive and absorbed in the relationship which makes the relationship incredibly enticing. Feelings of loneliness melt away. Many people share intimate feelings and thoughts with their affair partners; feeling understood and appreciated for the first time in a long time. This special connection often makes many people question their commitment to their marriages.

• **Boredom**

Sometimes the boredom isn't due to sexual boredom, but simply boredom or unhappiness with one's life, generically. A bored spouse could be in a dead end job, or feel overwhelmed with toddlers and family obligations, or be unhappy with their general choices in life. Then, in order to perk things up a bit, there is a search for novelty and excitement. Doing something illicit spices things up. Life seems fun and meaningful again.

• **For reassurance**

As we age, our bodies change. Many people feel insecure about the fact that they might not be as physically attractive as they once were. Discomfort with growing old can catapult people into a midlife crisis. If you're married to someone who is going through this intense period of questioning and existential angst, you'll be familiar with the following stereotypical red flags:

Exercising many hours a day

Losing weight

Buying a new, sexier and more youthful wardrobe

Purchasing new, outward signs of youth such as a "red convertible"

Blaming one's spouse for problems in the marriage

Hanging out with new, often younger (and single) people

Developing different interests in musical groups

Having plastic surgery

In an attempt to feel reassured that they are still sexy and attractive, many people flirt and have affairs. They enjoy the feeling of someone new "wanting" them because it's extremely validating.

- **Revenge sex**

Sometimes people have affairs to get back at their spouses because of a previous affair or some other unacceptable behavior. Revenge sex is supposed to make the betrayer feel more empowered and less like a victim. Punishment is often a motive. The revengeful spouse reasons, "If I retaliate and hurt my mate, I'll feel better because he will get a sense of how horribly his affair hurt me."

People who have revenge sex often feel justified if their spouses have had affairs. You've heard the old adage that two wrongs don't make a right. In my experience, this has been true. In fact, two wrongs simply double the trauma and difficulty in the marriage. Two wrongs don't even things out; it simply causes all hell to break loose.

- **Family history of infidelity**

If people grew up in families where there was infidelity, it may be viewed as the norm and it can be easier for them to choose to be unfaithful later in life. Most people are not necessarily aware of the connection between their decision to stray and their family history, but this doesn't negate the fact they can be inextricably connected.

That said, it's not as if being unfaithful is in our DNA and we are powerless to make good decisions due to childhood influences. We can create the lives we desire by becoming more conscious about our values and making certain our choices are in alignment with our values.

- **Sexual addiction**

Sometimes, an affair is not just an affair; it's a part of a sexual addiction. There is a difference between having one or two affairs and having a sexual addiction. Although the topic of sexual addiction is beyond the scope of this book, I want to give you a definition of it so that if you are concerned about this issue, you will get some additional help.

There is an excellent website with lots of free information about this topic. It's called recoverynation.com. Its founder, the late Jon Marsh, defines sexual addiction as the following: "Sexual addiction is nothing more than a continuing pattern of unwanted compulsive sexual behavior that has had a negative impact on an individual's personal, social and/or economic standing." It may include promiscuity, prostitutes, escorts, extensive use of pornography or masturbation, and so on.

Many addicts know that they are hurting themselves and the people they love but have no desire, motivation or know-how to stop. As with other addictions such as alcohol, many sexual addicts act out sexually to control a variety of unmanageable emotions. To break free of this cycle, the addict needs to learn new skills and put them to use in a consistent manner.

If you are concerned about a possible sexual addiction, you can take a survey on the aforementioned website to help you determine if you need additional help.

Now that you've given some thought to the possible reasons you decided to have an affair, it's time to move on to the next phase of this process- rebuilding.

PART III

REBUILDING

CHAPTER FIVE

MORE TASKS FOR THE BETRAYED SPOUSE

I F YOU ARE reading this chapter, I want to congratulate you. You are obviously serious about putting the past in the past and moving forward in your life. You want to feel better and closer to your spouse and you are doing the work to make that happen. That's fantastic. You should be really proud of yourself. I know I am proud of you.

I'm going to assume that you are working on the tasks I suggested in Chapter 3 and by now, you are noticing some improvements. If not, go back to Chapter 3 and keep practicing what I suggested there. Then proceed to this chapter.

Now that you've got some progress happening, I can share what you need to do to keep the "good stuff" happening, to keep forward motion in your marriage. At this juncture, I am assuming you've already let go of some of your most intense emotions and you're having some good times with your spouse. You now want things to be even better. So, are you ready? Well, I have some proven and workable ideas for you.

Identify what needs to change in your marriage

At this point in therapy, I will tell my clients, "Okay, you've made it through the first really tough phase! The intense hurt and rage has died down and you are having some good times together. Now I want to help you thrive." Then I say, "Now it's time to identify what needs to change or improve about your marriage." When I suggest this idea, I get one of two responses. Some people are eager to examine ways to tweak their marriages for the better, or even to undergo major overhauls. They realize that something has been missing and they truly want to put the effort into discovering the missing pieces and remedy the problems. There may be underlying issues (before and aside from the affair) that have eroded away at their marriage, and were never adequately addressed. There may be things they want to change about their spouses or that their spouses would like to change about them.

If problems in your marriage contributed to your spouse's feeling vulnerable to the affections of another person, it's important to address what was troubling him or her. Or perhaps your spouse has told you that everything in your marriage was fine, that the affair did not signal trouble in your relationship- it was an affair of impulsivity or curiosity – and not lack, or need. And this may absolutely be true. But my feeling is that even if your marriage was perfectly fine before the infidelity, it has not been fine recently, or you wouldn't have picked up this book. The affair has created new problems between you. Therefore, this is a great opportunity to fix what has been broken, either before, during or after the affair. In fact, as I have assured you many times now, it really is possible for you to have an even better relationship than ever before.

Once people begin feeling the benefits of working out their problems, they often say that the affair was a blessing in disguise. Now, I know this might not sound plausible to you right now, especially if feelings are still raw and tender, but believe me, with the passage of time and proactive work, this is possible. That's because the affair forces people to tackle issues in a more thorough, open and transparent way than they've ever done in the past.

The second response I receive when I ask a couple to identify what needs to change about the marriage after the affair is one of defensiveness. It usually sounds something like this, "The only thing that needs to change is for my spouse to be faithful. He or she created this problem. I don't need to change anything. Don't blame me- I'm the victim here."

This sort of thinking may feel justified, but it won't get you anywhere. You have to be willing to take an honest look at your marriage and assess ways to make it stronger. This might include things that you need to do differently too. Why not ensure the best possible outcome by exploring all ways to make your marriage great?

Start by asking yourself, "What would make my marriage even better than it was before the affair?" I really want you to visualize what the two of you would be doing, and what your marriage would look like on a daily basis, if your marriage were better than ever.

Now, think about what would need to change in order to feel really happy with your partner, so that your marriage is the best it's ever been. Do you need to spend more time together? Do you need to talk about important issues more regularly? Do you need help learning how to co-parent more cooperatively? Do you need to put some focus and energy back on loving touch, flirting and sensuality in your relationship? Do you need to simply pay more attention to each other? If you feel you've had a child-centered marriage, is it time to re-orient your lives so that your marriage is more central? Do you need new skills to learn how to argue constructively?

When you consider these questions, make sure that your responses are action-oriented; describe what you and your spouse will be *doing* differently when you are accomplishing these goals. Although I have given you examples of what I mean by "action-oriented goals" in other sections of this book, I want to go over it once again and make it very clear. It's a step that can't be rushed over or missed, and is vital to recovery and re-creating a better-than-ever marriage.

Instead of saying, "I want to feel more trust in you," say, "I need you to continue letting me know about your whereabouts so I feel safe." Similarly, rather than saying, "I need more attention from you," say, "I still want you to come home an hour earlier from work as you have been doing. That gives us more time together in the evening and I like that." Instead of telling your spouse, "I need you to be reassuring," say, "It really helps when you tell me why you love me and why you want to stay in this marriage." Be concrete and specific. Talk action!

Once you have figured out what you'd like to improve about your marriage, it's time to share your thoughts with your spouse. When you do, make sure that you speak in such a way that he or she doesn't feel blamed. You can do this by using "I-messages." When you use I-messages, you take responsibility for your thoughts, perspectives and feelings. They are non-blaming sentences. I-messages allow others to hear what you have to say without becoming defensive. Here's an example.

Say, "I would like to talk more often," instead of saying, "You never want to talk to me." Say, "I feel hurt when you spend so much time on the computer," instead of saying, "You never get off the computer. It's the only thing you really care about." Say, "I'd like it if you'd agree to spend more time with my family," instead of saying, "You don't care about my family or my feelings."

Get the picture?

It also helps to ask for what you want, rather than tell your spouse what you're unhappy about. Asking for what you want in the future is a request for change. Saying what you're unhappy about is a complaint about the past. We can't change the past, but we can change the future. This is a more optimistic approach, and you'll discover that making a habit of saying what you like and want, rather than criticizing what you don't like or want, will yield wonderfully positive results. It takes practice because the default mode of most people is to focus on and complain about what's bothering them. But with intention and practice, you can change what comes naturally!

For example, say, "I'd like it if you would be more involved with the kid's after-school activities," rather than, "I feel like I'm a single parent most of the time. You never help with after-school activities." Or say, "I'd like you to do the planning for our date nights every other week," instead of, "I'm always the one to arrange date nights." Get the idea?

If you have trouble identifying what you want to change or improve about your marriage, I have a suggestion. Ask yourself the following question:

"If you went to sleep tonight and a miracle happened, so that everything you've been upset about totally disappeared while you were sleeping, how would your day unfold?" Remember, this occurred during your sleep and no one told you there was a miracle, it just happened. What would be going on when you woke up tomorrow morning that let you believe that a true miracle took place? What would you and your spouse be *doing* differently from the moment you woke up? (de Shazer, 1988)

Don't rush this question. For most of my clients, the "miracle question" is a game-changer, in a good way. Close your eyes for a moment and imagine that this miracle happened. And you and your spouse wake up from a good night's sleep. What would happen next? Would you stay in bed and snuggle for a while? Would you kiss each other good morning? Would you get up and have coffee together and discuss your days. Once your day has started, what would happen next? Would you spend the day together or not? Would you have contact during the day? What form would this contact take? What would you do in the evening?

After you describe your miracle day in great detail, even writing it down, think about your life in a broader way. What would you like to do as a couple that you haven't been doing so much lately? What is on your marital bucket list? What would make your marriage much more satisfying and fun and passionate? What would make you really, really glad you stayed to work things out?

Here are some other helpful questions to ask yourself.

After the miracle happened, what would those closest to you- your children, friends and family- notice about the two of you that would be different? How could they tell that this miracle had happened in your lives? Would they notice you being more affectionate with one another, laughing more, spending more time together, getting along much better? What would they see that would clue them in that something truly different is happening?

As you answer these questions, you should also ask yourself, "Are small parts of the miracle actually already happening? If so, what are they?" Take time to appreciate how far you've come from the beginning stages of this process.

And now to the challenging part of recovery, healing and improving your marriage. You need to be honest with yourself about areas of improvement that your spouse wants and needs to be different. But how do you do that? Begin by asking yourself, "What has my spouse complained about in the past?" What has been a source of disagreement between the two of you? Where have you hit stalemates in your marriage?

Now, when you think about these questions, keep in mind, that you don't have to agree with your spouse's assessment of the problems in your marriage. He or she might be over-reacting. But it doesn't change the fact that your spouse might have been unhappy, felt that you didn't understand the importance of his or her wants, needs and desires.

Have you ever held strong emotions about something that mattered a great deal to you, and then felt the sting of someone's lack or caring, unwillingness to change, or inability to validate your feelings? This is the way your mate feels, too, when you refuse to acknowledge their emotions in a caring way, and do what you can to help or change.

So, back to the question. What has your spouse requested in the past that you didn't deem important at the time? Was it more sex, more physical closeness, emotional connection, time together, independent time, help around the house, collaboration around issues pertaining to the kids, extended family, financial matters, drug or alcohol use, or health issues? Contemplate it, and if possible, write it down.

Once you identify what your spouse's concerns have been, you need to make a commitment to do something about them. As I say this, I can imagine you wondering why you "have to do all the work." Trust me, you won't be doing all the work. I will be expecting your spouse to take the same inventory and identify areas he or she needs to change. Plus, it's been my experience that once one person extends the olive branch and works hard at pleasing the other spouse, the other spouse reciprocates in big ways. That's how relationships improve, through mutual care-taking. In fact, this is a good time for me to say a little more about mutual care-taking.

In my work, I have discovered that people tend to give to their spouse in the way they like to receive. But that's not real giving.

Real giving is when you give your partner the things *your partner* wants and needs, whether or not you like it, agree with it or completely understand it. You do it because loving relationships are built on this sort of mutual care-taking.

I'd like to share an example with you out of my own life. One of my definitions of real giving came from my early relationship with my mother with whom I was very close. When I was young and I came home from a bad day at school, my intuitive mother could always tell something was wrong. Then she showed me her love and caring by talking to me about my day, asking me many questions.

"Michele, did something go wrong at school today? Did you have a problem with a teacher, a friend or on the playground? Did something go wrong on a test? What happened? I can tell you're upset."

So, I associated love with someone asking questions about how I felt.

I took this lesson about love and caring into the early years of my relationship with my husband, Jim. He was a real estate developer. And I could tell when he had a hard day just by the look on his face when he arrived home. So, I showed my loving concern by asking him lots of questions. "Jim, what went wrong today? Was it one of your employees? Did a contract fall through? Is something going wrong with the construction? Is there a sales problem?" And on and on.

I thought I was being incredibly loving and doing real giving. But apparently, my "gift" was returned unopened. Jim didn't see my questions in the same light. In fact, he felt annoyed by them. He didn't want to rehash his day and preferred to work things out on his own...silently.

I finally figured out that if I truly wanted to do some "real giving" to my husband, I would have to give him space and *NOT talk*. This response seemed completely unnatural, it defied every bone in my body.

I came to realize that often, when what you're doing feels unnatural, it's a good thing; it means you're doing real giving. You're doing what works for your partner, not for you. You're stretching outside your comfort zone to help your partner in his or her way, not yours. And to that I now say, "Congratulations!"

I started teaching couples about the importance of real giving and discovered a wonderful resource on this topic. It's a book called, THE FIVE LOVE LANGUAGES, by Gary Chapman. In it, Dr. Chapman details five love languages, or five different ways people feel loved by others. I suggest you read it, but I will give you a short description of his thoughts.

Dr. Chapman believes there are five primary love languages. He thinks people feel loved through:

- Time Together- when their partner spends quality time with them

- Words of Affirmation- through encouraging words and meaningful conversations

- Receiving Gifts- when they receive material gifts from their spouse

- Acts of Service- when their spouse does things such as cleaning the house, taking care of the kids, warming a car before traveling on a cold wintry evening, taking the clothes to the cleaners, bringing coffee to them and so on

- Physical Touch- through sexual, affectionate, or sensual touch of any kind

As you read through the different love languages, can you identify yours? What are your top two love languages? In order for you to feel loved, your spouse needs to connect with you in those particular ways, or "love languages." Now, what are your spouse's top two love languages? What do *you* need to do to help him or her feel loved? If you're having trouble identifying your love languages, here is a helpful online resource. It's an inventory you can take on Dr. Gary Chapman's website.

Once you identify what you think are your spouse's top two love languages, check with your mate to see if you guessed correctly. Did you? If so, great. If not, ask your spouse to talk to you about why he or she chose that particular love language.

Now, what I'd like for you to do is to grade yourself on an "A-F" scale (with an "A" being excellent, and an "F" being a failing grade) on how well you have shown love *in your partner's* love language. In other words, if your partner chose "Touch" as their top love language, how important has your sexual relationship been in your lives? How often do you cuddle together or kiss and hug each other? Do you walk arm in arm when you walk together?

Similarly, if your spouse said that "Acts of Service" is their top love language, do you do a good job fixing things around the house, taking care of the kids, cooking, doing errands, handling finances and so on?

How well have you been showing love in your spouse's love language? If you've done a great job, that's fantastic. Most of the people I work with give themselves fairly low grades. In other words, there's lots of room for improvement. Be honest with yourself. If your spouse's love language is "touch" and there hasn't been a lot of physical contact, whether or not it's a priority to you, touch has to become more important in your lives together.

But this isn't just a one-way street. I am going to ask your spouse to take the same inventory and grade him or herself on how well your spouse has done in terms of speaking *your* love language over the years. If your spouse hasn't initiated conversation about love languages, feel free to bring it up. I am going to ask him or her to read this chapter, but you may get to this topic at different times because one of you reads faster than the other. It doesn't matter who starts the discussion about love languages, it just matters that you talk about it.

Now, ask yourself what you specifically need to think or do differently to raise your love languages grade. Ask yourself, "What do I need to do to move from a 'C' to a 'B' to demonstrate my love in my spouse's love language?" As always, be specific and concrete. (By now, you know I will be looking for observable actions! No fuzzy, nondescript, generic feelings. Tell me what you will do differently, what your spouse would see and experience when you start speaking their language?)

If your spouse's love language is "Time Together," and work has been a major focus for you, perhaps you need to come home earlier each day or spend less time on work-related activities in the evening or on the weekends. Maybe you need to take more initiative in dreaming up ideas and planning date nights, or a special weekend getaway, or arranging for babysitters.

You see, if you want your marriage to be great, your spouse has to feel loved. And the best way for this to happen is to speak your partner's love language like a pro.

People often think that working on relationships is hard work. I don't believe that people have to work harder to get better results, they have to work smarter. Working smarter means at least two things. First, it means knowing your partner's love languages and showing love in those ways. Secondly, it means understanding the following important relationship principle.

When your needs aren't being met in your marriage, the default reaction is to half your efforts to please the other person. In short, you most likely think, "If I'm not happy, I'm not going to go out of my way to make *you* happy." Make no bones about it, this is exactly how marriages fail.

Even though you may feel hurt or even rejected, if you want to change the dynamics in your marriage you've got to take the high road. Muster up the energy to be loving towards your spouse even when you're feeling short-changed. Be willing to be the "first domino" that falls and initiates change. This is where the rubber meets the road. It's essential that you put yourself out and show love (in your partner's love language), even when you feel like he or she doesn't deserve it. Sounds crazy, right? Let me explain why, as "unnatural" as this may feel, it is the brilliant relational step to make.

Let's say that the husband's love language is "touch" and the wife's language is "time together." She is only "naturally" interested in being physically intimate when they are close emotionally, or when they've spent quality time together. If he's been busy with work and inattentive, she doesn't want to have sex at all.

He feels loved through touch. If she isn't willing to have sex at all, he feels hurt and rejected. He withdraws from the relationship and the "quality time together" doesn't happen. Instead, he spends extra hours at work to distract himself from feeling sexually rejected. The more he works, the less she feels like touching him. The less she touches him, the more he avoids her. It's the classic Catch-22!

Then what's the solution to this? *Both* people need to take responsibility for change! She needs to reach out to him physically, even if he seems preoccupied or irritable. It will soften his heart and make him want to be with her. He needs to spend more time with her, even if he's feeling rejected sexually. It will please her and make her want to be closer to him physically.

Neither person will really feel in the mood to reach out at first, but for a marriage to thrive, both partners have to stretch outside their comfort zones. And the best part of all of this is that when you reach out, not only will you please your spouse, but your spouse will want to please you. It's a win-win situation, as all good marriage interactions should be.

Once you start showing love in your spouse's love language, you should monitor your progress. It helps to ask yourself the following scaling questions. They are similar to the scaling questions you asked yourself in Chapter 3.

On a 1 to 10 scale, with 10 being great and one being the pits, where on the scale would you have rated yourself when you discovered the affair?

On this same scale, where would you rate yourself in the last few weeks? (You might have to average the weeks to get a general number.)

Given that things are never perfect, where on the scale would you have to be to feel like things are truly working between you and your spouse?

What might be one or two things you could do or that could happen in the next few weeks that would bring you a half step closer to your goal?

You should ask yourself these scaling questions regularly so that you can get a sense about the progress you are making. When you answer these questions in a clear and concrete way, it will give you a specific plan for what you and your spouse need to do next.

By the way, if you have determined that a source of unhappiness for your spouse has been your sexual relationship, eventually you will need to address this. You may or may not be ready to do this. You may have experienced some false starts trying to resume your sex life with your partner. Perhaps you can't stop thinking about the affair or you have had flashbacks. I will help you with that in Chapter 7. But for now, just realize that a loving, passionate sexual relationship is an important part of every healthy marriage. This applies to your marriage as well.

One thing to keep in mind: when you are discussing what needs to change in your marriage, don't think that you have to tackle everything all at once. Take your time. Don't get overwhelmed or overwhelm your spouse. Hopefully, you will have a lifetime together to shape and re-shape your marriage as necessary. Address one or two issues at a reasonable pace. Work on changing one or two areas that most needs to change first. Assess how you are doing by having regular conversations about the state of the marriage. Set aside specific times to talk, preferably in a peaceful environment and when you are both well-rested. Get additional help if your conversations continually spiral out of control or head into destructive places.

The most important thing is to remain open and honest about your feelings. Honesty is the antidote to the bad feelings left in the wake of the affair. Being transparent and upfront will help you both feel close, putting you on the same team again.

Deal constructively with intermittent anger or negative feelings

In Chapter 3, I told you that it was very important to identify your emotions and to let your spouse know when you're feeling angry, sad, rage, confused, devastated and so on. Although I think it is important to keep the lines of communication open, there also comes a time when you need to consider the impact that hearing negative feelings has on your spouse.

For example, if your spouse is working really hard on the marriage and on him or herself, it's hard to constantly be reminded of past mistakes. Your spouse wants to begin to put the past where it belongs. Gradually, it will help if you can find new ways to deal with your feelings when they arise, ways that might not include talking to your spouse.

For instance, when you're feeling badly, you might consider speaking to a trusted friend or family member about your emotions. Just be sure that your confidante will support your marriage even though you might be having a rough patch. (Often, the best advisors are those who have been through a similar issue in their marriage, but worked through it, and went on to enjoy a marriage that thrived. Choose someone who can show that balance of compassion for your current feelings, while also championing your marriage.) Your spouse may need a little break from the frequent conversations about what happened. It's not that you can never discuss your feelings; it's just that it might be time to pare down the frequency.

If what I'm saying resonates with you, you are probably ready to slow down your conversations about the affair. That's a good thing. If, on the other hand, you're saying to yourself, "I need to be able to talk about things when I'm upset," then you are probably not quite ready to curb these discussions. Follow your instincts, but understand that the ultimate goal is to eventually talk less about what happened and more about your future together.

Let your spouse know what he or she is doing right

In addition to cutting back on the conversations about the affair, make sure you let your spouse know when you notice when they are putting effort into working on the marriage. Positively reinforce your spouse's attempts to do what is outlined in this book. I've seen lots of couples struggle with this. The unfaithful spouse is truly remorseful and works really hard to create trust, but those behaviors are taken for granted. Unfaithful spouses are often starved for a few encouraging words.

If, over time, the unfaithful spouse is putting forth a lot of effort, but never receives encouragement, they will become discouraged and feel like giving up. You don't want your spouse to stop engaging in healing behaviors. You want those good things to continue. That's why positive reinforcement is so important.

If your spouse has been patient and honest most of the time, even when it has been difficult, let them know that you noticed their efforts. Tell them, "I appreciate how hard you are working on things. I appreciate your listening to me, even when it's challenging." Or, "When you agreed to talk last night even though you weren't in the mood, it meant a lot to me." Your spouse wants you to feel better and it helps to let them know when they are getting it right.

Some people are hesitant to let their spouses know when things are going well because they're afraid it will let them off the hook, or that their spouses will actually stop trying once they feel like they are "on safer ground" with the betrayed spouse. Here's what I discovered about that.

Positive reinforcement is the best way to encourage someone to keep doing what they're doing. Not only that, but if your spouse has been consistent in working hard on your marriage, praise is deserved. So, don't be stingy with it. Affirmation will help your spouse to keep on keeping on.

One more thing you need to know if you are withholding praise because you are worried that all of your spouse's efforts will come to a screeching halt if they believe the problems have subsided. Although this might be hard for you to believe, your spouse probably feels really good about the reparative actions they are taking. Behaviors such as spending more time with the kids, doing one's fair share of household chores, prioritizing their marriage, being more patient with loved ones, not only improves your relationship, but it also restores your spouse's self-esteem. Doing the "right things" just feels good, and that's incredibly reinforcing.

That's why many unfaithful spouses say, "Even if our marriage doesn't work out, I will continue to be this new person because I like myself much more now." This means that your spouse isn't just "being on their best behavior" temporarily as a ploy to win back your heart, your spouse has turned over a new leaf.

That said, it's safe for you to acknowledge the positive changes you see without concern that your spouse's new behaviors will vanish into thin air. They won't, rest assured that change is here to stay.

Be empathetic

When you found out about the affair, you were probably so hurt that you had almost no ability to understand your mate's actions or feel any empathy for them. But at some point, it will help both you and your spouse when you try to feel compassion and empathy.

You might be wondering what I mean by this. If your spouse had an affair because he or she was unhappy or felt neglected, you don't have to condone the affair in any way to show understanding for the reasons your spouse strayed. This doesn't mitigate the impact of the choice your spouse made, but it means you've been able to take a step back and see the bigger picture.

For example, if your spouse felt neglected because they believed you put the children first and didn't prioritize the marriage, you can acknowledge your spouse's yearning for closeness and any emotional void they may have felt at the time. While at the same time, both of you understand that there were better ways to deal with marital dissatisfaction.

Similarly, if your spouse had a parent who was unfaithful throughout his or her childhood, it might be somewhat easier to understand how this sort of upbringing could lead someone to making similar choices.

Along those same lines, if your spouse was struggling with self-esteem issues and feeling less than sexy, proving that he or she was still attractive might have been the reason your spouse strayed.

In short, although you never wanted an affair to happen, you might be more able to understand the conditions that added up to your spouse's choice to have an affair. Realizing that no one is perfect and everyone makes mistakes, you may be feeling a bit less angry and somewhat more empathetic.

I truly believe that if your spouse had known a better way to deal with the feelings they were battling, your spouse would have made better choices. The late poet and philosopher, Maya Angelou once said, "People do the best they can with the tools they have. If they knew better, they would do better." I am convinced Maya Angelou was right.

Have you found yourself softening a bit in your outlook towards your spouse? Have you told yourself that, although this has been hurtful beyond anything you've experienced before, your spouse's remorse has been real, and encouraging? Have you been making more of an effort to see things through your spouse's eyes?

I'm assuming you have been seeing your spouse in a different, more positive light lately. If you haven't, it may mean that you are still at the stage in the healing process where you are focusing on your hurt, not yet able to step back and see the bigger picture.

Unfortunately, it's hard to extend generosity to your spouse until you feel like you are standing on solid emotional ground. If this is where you are, keep working at nurturing yourself and asking for what you need from your spouse. Time (and consistent effort) will help melt the harshness you might be feeling towards your spouse.

Do thought-stopping

If you're like most people who have been betrayed, you have probably ruminated and ruminated and ruminated some more. It's easy to get stuck in a rut thinking about negative or unsettling things on an on-going basis. Rumination might have caused sleep problems or an inability to function during the day.

Hopefully, you are doing less and less of that by now. Still, you are likely to find that intrusive thoughts can get in the way of your being present in your relationship or in your life in general.

In Chapter 3, I shared that intrusive thoughts are perfectly normal after the revelation of an affair, and to just allow the feelings to arise. However, you may want to have more control over when you allow these thoughts to surface, and how to keep them from spiraling out of control. It's a technique called thought-stopping.

Although there are different ways to practice thought-stopping, here's a strategy that has worked for many people in my practice. It goes like this. Once you read the directions, you may feel more at peace closing your eyes and doing this exercise. Find yourself a comfortable place to sit. Take a few deep breaths.

I want you to call to mind an image of a safe, serene, comfortable place. It can be a place in nature, a person with whom you love to spend time, or any situation that has offered you peacefulness in the past. I want you to really allow yourself to get into the feeling that arises when you are calm and connected to this place of comfort. Picture the situation or person in great detail. Use all the senses. See the image clearly. Hear the sounds around you. Smell the smells. Immerse yourself into this calm, safe picture.

Once you are in your "happy place," ponder the exact thought that has been distressing and repetitive. Now, I would like for you to imagine a big, red stop sign. Say to yourself, "Stop!" Then switch your mental channel back to the peaceful place you conjured to mind just moments earlier. Allow yourself to remain there.

Then, each time random distressing thoughts arise, repeat the exercise. Imagine the stop sign; then go to your place of safety and comfort. This isn't easy to do, especially at first. But with practice, you can get more control over chasing away intrusive thoughts. You have to commit to doing this on a regular basis to feel the positive effects of choosing what your focus will be. Gaining some mastery over your own mind during a crisis like this will also have positive ripple results in every area of your life in the future.

Stop snooping

By now, I hope you have more faith in your spouse and if you had been snooping or prying, that you have stopped that behavior. It isn't good for you. It only makes you feel badly. Even if your spouse has been doing nothing wrong, you may still be suspicious, wondering if your mate has just learned to hide the misdeeds more efficiently. Perhaps, they just have not been caught. Yet. So, you spend energy spying a bit more meticulously. Though it can be a natural reflex after feeling "duped" in the past; perpetual spying behavior isn't helpful to your healing.

If you're still snooping, it will keep you trapped in thinking about the affair, which is no way to live. Eventually, you will need to tell yourself to lighten up and let go. Hopefully, you are starting to see some signs that perpetual scrutiny isn't necessary and it feels better to assume honesty and integrity on the part of your spouse.

Don't mind read

Amy and Matt are a couple I worked with after Matt had a two-year affair with a co-worker. Our work together was successful and they were well on the way to repairing their marriage. But they kept hitting the same bump in the road.

Matt had given up his affair long before I met them and they were having really good times together, making great progress. However, each time Matt was pensive or withdrawn, Amy immediately assumed he was thinking about his affair partner and regretting his decision to end the affair.

To cast some doubt into her unhelpful thinking, I asked Amy, "How can you tell the difference between times when Matt might be thinking of that woman and times when he's quiet, simply because he's often quiet, or he's thinking about work, the kids, or some other part of his life?" After reflecting on my question, she admitted that she really didn't know how to answer me. She realized that she was doing a lot of assuming and second-guessing. Simply because she had these automatic responses did not mean her thoughts were true. In fact, the preponderance of evidence pointed to quite the opposite

In short, Amy was mindreading. Here's the truth about

mindreading. No one can do it. Sometimes, we think we can do it. But sometimes, we're wrong. I told Amy, "I understand your feelings, but it would be much more therapeutic for you to simply ask Matt what he's thinking when he grows quiet. And remember, that Matt's personality has been on the withdrawn side, ever since you've know him, long before the affair."

So, don't mind read. Don't assume you know what your spouse is thinking. You will probably be thinking the worst and that will only make your life unhappy. It is understandable that you might worry from time to time about your spouse's lingering feelings for the affair partner, but every moment of quietude is not an indication that your spouse is pining away.

It is easy for your fears to drive your thoughts unless you take over the mental wheel. Tell yourself that you're over-reacting. Learn to turn down the volume on the voices that make you feel badly. Remind yourself that your spouse has been working hard at making the marriage a happier place for both of you. Use that stop sign and switch to your happy place!

Regain your self-esteem

As I told you in Chapter 3, infidelity often makes the betrayed spouse feel that their self-esteem has taken a big hit. As the betrayed partner, you've probably worried about your attractiveness, your lovability, your sexiness, and your ability to please your partner. You undoubtedly have compared yourself to your spouse's affair partner and wondered what they had, that you didn't have, that lured your spouse away?

Hopefully, you are doing less of this kind of thinking these days. But if you're still struggling with feeling good about yourself, it is time to pull out the big guns and get serious about loving yourself again.

I'd like to recommend a resource for you if you enjoy reading. A friend and colleague, Steven Stosny, wrote an excellent book entitled, LIVING & LOVING AFTER BETRAYAL: HOW TO HEAL FROM EMOTIONAL ABUSE, DECEIT, INFIDELITY AND CHRONIC RESENTMENT. It's all about how the betrayed spouse can find ways to heal from within. It's an excellent guide for learning skills to self-nurture. It will help you find your center again.

In Chapter 3, I offered a list of things many people in your shoes do to feel better. Have you been actively pursuing activities that bring you joy and peace? Have you been focusing on what's good in your life instead of the pain you've experienced? Do you feel gratitude for the things that are going well right now? Have you taken to heart what's good about you and the person you really are inside? Are you beginning to see that your spouse's decision to stray was not a comment about you, but rather a choice he or she made independently? You are still the same wonderful person you were before the affair. Nothing your spouse has done- or not done- can change that. In fact, you may want to copy this paragraph and put it somewhere that you can read it every day, to keep focused on your progress and who you really are as a person. This is especially true when you feel yourself starting to sink back in the mire of low-self-image or intrusive and painful thought loops.

If you still have lingering feelings of low self-worth because of what happened, it is time for you to make sure you are receiving help to feel better. You need to take responsibility for feeling happy with who you are. Your spouse must certainly help in big ways, but again, in the end, you have to be in charge of you. In his book, LIVING AND LOVING AFTER BETRAYAL, Dr. Stosny writes,

It may seem patently unfair that the injured party in an intimate betrayal has to take responsibility for her (or his) personal healing. That's because healing has nothing to do with fairness; it has to do with power. Where blame renders us powerless, responsibility empowers. (pg. 41)

Then Dr. Stosny offers a worthwhile exercise that helps people develop a healing rather than a victim mentality.

Take a moment to think about your most recent bad mood. List three things that might have caused it (For example: thinking about the betrayal, trouble with family members or friends and friction at work).

Indicate who is to blame for each item you listed above. If the blame is egregious, write "a lot" next to the name.

Now take three minutes to write down what you can do to improve the things that triggered your bad mood. Time yourself. Stop writing after three minutes, whether you have come up with something or not.

This exercise will help you take control of your emotions and your life, something you (and everyone) needs to do.

Forgive

Ultimately, if you are going to live the rest of your life in peace and harmony, you will want to find a way to forgive your partner about the affair, especially if he or she is making amends. Depending on the timing of when you are reading this, you may or may not be ready to consider forgiveness. Some people forgive too quickly, without doing the necessary work to get things back on track. This is not advisable. On the other hand, others find it hard to ever forgive.

I believe that forgiveness is not something you do for others; it's actually a gift you give yourself. If you have been holding on to a grudge, it affects your life in drastic ways. When you wake up in the morning, it casts a gray shadow over everything you see. Your life is no longer in Technicolor. There's a low-grade depression that lies just below the surface. It wreaks havoc with your immune system and the way you feel physically; you're tired, burned out, you feel a lack of motivation. Life feels sad.

You may try putting these feelings of lingering resentment in a box, but they are constantly a thorn in your side. Bitterness and residual anger carry more weight than you have even realized. They rob you of a full passionate life.

Plus, if you have children, know that they are watching you and your spouse. They're learning about love and marriage (and forgiveness) through observing your actions. If you are distant and cold because you are unable to let go of resentments, you have to ask yourself, "Is this the lesson about love I want my children to take into their future relationships? Is this what I want them to know about caring, love and connection?"

Additionally, we all know the adage that life is short. Do you really want to spend the rest of your precious life feeling bitter, or do you want to rise above and feel better? Even if you were to decide to leave your marriage, you can't escape the pain of the betrayal. Here's the truth: you'd have to work through the betrayal and its aftermath, with or without your spouse. A divorce just increases the number of emotional challenges you have to tackle. It doesn't make life simpler.

Sometimes, when I talk to couples about the importance of forgiveness, betrayed spouses tell me, "Here's the deal: I'm afraid that if I forgive my spouse, it would condone what happened. And I cannot do that with a sense of integrity."

So let me reassure you: forgiveness is not about condoning someone's behavior. You're not saying that you agree with what happened and that you're letting your spouse off the hook. You are still holding your spouse accountable, but you are choosing to focus on the fact that no one is perfect, not even you. And since people make mistakes, forgiveness is often warranted. It allows everyone to start over. It feels good.

Other times, betrayed spouses say, "I can't forgive because I can't forget." Forgiveness should not be confused with forgetting. You can't forget what happened. In fact, you *shouldn't* forget what happened. It is wonderful that people can learn from the past and their mistakes. You both need to learn what to do, and what not to do, to keep your marriage healthy.

Though it is unrealistic to assume that you will ever forget what happened, here's what I have learned from couples who have successfully healed from infidelity.

Memories of the affair begin to occur less and less frequently. And when they do happen, the intensity with which people experience emotions tends to shift dramatically over time. Each thought about the betrayal carries with it less of a sting, especially if you work through it as suggested in this book. Until eventually, unmanageable emotions fade.

When I tell you that forgiveness is a gift you give yourself, I mean it. You are no longer shackled by the past. You are no longer a prisoner of negativity and blame. Your heart is open to positive experiences. You're emotionally present. It's easier to give and to receive. Forgiveness is the gift you give yourself after all the hard work you have been doing to repair your marriage and also to nourish and nurture yourself. Letting go is life-giving.

If you can't think about forgiveness yet without feeling a strong, almost visceral reaction, it probably means that you have more healing to do. Many professionals say that you can't heal unless you forgive. But I think this is backward. People forgive more easily *after they have healed*. Forgiveness follows healing, not the other way around. You have to know that you are okay before you grant forgiveness to your partner.

So, if forgiveness has not been on your short list of things to do, it probably means that you need to slow down a bit and review the tasks outlined in Chapter 3. Be compassionate with yourself, regardless of where you might be in this healing journey. Many therapists say that it takes a full two years for people to transform their marriages after an affair. I think that no two couples are alike; some heal more quickly and others take more time. Don't judge yourself if you aren't where you had hoped you would be by now. It is what it is. Just keep working your plan and eventually, things will get better.

One more thing, healing comes to people in much the way Spring follows Winter. You will experience a warm day here and there, followed by a reprisal of Winter's cold. But over time, you get a few more warm days closer together, and eventually you realize that you've finally lived into Spring, where there are more warm, sunny days than rainy or dreary ones.

An alternative to forgiveness- acceptance.

But what if you are someone who can't see yourself being able to forgive your spouse? Perhaps your spouse's actions belie your own morals and core values in such a way that you simply can't forgive him or her. There is an alternative. It's called acceptance.

When your spouse's actions have truly violated principles that are your guiding light in life, it might be difficult to forgive him or her. However, you don't want to spend days, months or years wishing that the past hadn't been the past. You can't talk about what happened without becoming extremely emotional. Time hasn't dulled the pain.

Sometimes, in order to move forward, you can simply accept that an affair is now part of your personal and marital history together. You can do it matter-of-factly, the way you would have to accept any sad, life-altering experience. You do have to learn how to weave the tapestry of your life in a new way, a way that includes the story of infidelity. You have to be able to understand how the betrayal has changed you and your partner and how you are moving on together to a brighter future, with or without forgiveness. If, that is, you ever hope to live lightly and freely, with joy again.

I'd like to give you a personal example here. It isn't about infidelity, but it is about a part of my past that I had a great deal of difficulty accepting. I simply couldn't wrap my brain around it. And because I held on to wanting to change the past, I remained stuck; I couldn't move on with my life.

My mother and I had an extremely close relationship. We were joined at the hip. In many ways, she was my best friend. And then the unspeakable happened. She was driving a friend to the airport early one morning and hit some black ice. Her car hit a guardrail and she was killed on impact. She was in perfect health and had the mind of a steel trap. In a moment, without warning, without my knowing, I lost her.

For years, I played over and over in my mind what I should or could have done differently. For years, I couldn't believe that this nonsensical tragedy had actually happened and that she was gone. For years, I couldn't stop grieving or thinking that I would eventually wake up from this terrible nightmare. For years, a big part of my life was on hold.

But then, for a variety of reasons, I started to accept what had actually happened. I started to surrender to what happened. I began to focus on the blessings of having had her as my mother and the times we shared together. And slowly, but surely, I began to climb out of my dark place. My acceptance of what happened began to free me.

Now, I know that losing a loved one through accidental death is not the same thing as being betrayed by your spouse through an intentional act. I know it's different. But I also know that acceptance of things we cannot control is our ticket to inner peace. Holding on to the past or wishing things weren't so, is a formula for misery. Gautama Buddha once said, "Attachment leads to suffering." I believe this. Sure, there is a time to grieve what you wanted life to be, or what it might have been. Tears must rise and fall. But there comes a day that you decide to live again, and to do so you must let old dreams fade so that new dreams can come to your heart again.

If you are still having difficulty accepting what has happened in your life, I suggest you read the book, HOW CAN I FORGIVE YOU? by Janis Abrahms Springs, Ph.D. It will help.

Getting additional professional help

If, after reading this chapter, you don't feel ready to make some of the changes outlined, you might just need to be patient. You may need more time. Or, it might be time for you and your spouse to get some additional professional help. I'd like to offer your some advice about seeking help.

- Make sure your therapist has received specific training and is experienced in Marital therapy.

    Marital therapy requires very different skills than doing individual therapy. Individual therapists usually help people identify and process their inner feelings. They help people understand how the past is influencing the present. They assist them in achieving *personal* goals.

Couples therapists, on the other hand, need to be skilled at helping people overcome the differences that naturally occur when two people live under the same roof. They need to know what makes a marriage tick. A therapist can be very skilled as an individual therapist and be clueless about helping couples change. For this reason, don't be shy. Ask your therapist about his or her training and experience.

- In addition to making sure that your therapist is trained in couples therapy, you should also ascertain how much experience your therapist has had working with couples who have experienced infidelity. In particular, you'll want to know what percentage of the time the therapist has been able to help couples mend their marriage after the betrayal.

- Make sure your therapist is biased in the direction of helping you find solutions to your marital problems rather than helping you leave your marriage when things get rocky. Feel free to ask your therapist. "Under what circumstances would you believe that divorce is a viable alternative?" Your therapist's response will be very revealing.

- You should feel comfortable and respected by your therapist. You should feel that he or she understands your perspective and feelings. If your therapist sides with you or your spouse, that's not good. No one should feel ganged up on. If you aren't comfortable with something your therapist is suggesting- like setting a deadline to make a decision about your marriage- say so. If your therapist honors your feedback, that's a good sign. If not, leave.

- The therapist's own values about relationships definitely play a part in what he or she focuses on when working with you. Since there are few universal rules for being and staying in love, if your therapist insists that there is only one way to have a successful marriage, find another therapist.

Also, although some people think that their therapist is able to tell when a person should stop trying to work on their marriage, therapists really don't have this sort of knowledge. If they say things like, "It seems that you are incompatible," or "Why are you willing to put up with this,?" or "It is time to move on with your life," they are simply laying their own values on you. This is an unethical act, in my opinion.

- Make sure you (and your partner) and your therapist set concrete goals early on. If you don't, you will probably meet each week with no clear direction. Once you set goals, you should never lose sight of them. If you don't begin to see some progress within two or three sessions, you should address your concern with your therapist.

- It's my belief that couples in crisis don't have the luxury to analyze how they were raised in order to find solutions to their marital problems. If your therapist is focusing on the past, suggest a future-orientation. If he or she isn't willing to take your lead, find a therapist who will.

- Most of all, trust your instincts. If your therapist is helping, you'll know it. If he or she isn't, you'll know that too. Don't stay with a therapist who is just helping you tread water. Find one who will help you swim.

- Finally, the best way to find a good therapist is word-of-mouth. Satisfied customers say a lot about the kind of therapy you will receive. Although you might feel embarrassed to ask friends or family for a referral, you should consider doing it anyway. It increases the odds you'll find a therapist who will really help you and your spouse.

So don't give up on therapy, give up on bad therapy. You be the judge. There's a lot to be gained from seeking the advice from someone who can help you find simple solutions to life's complicated problems.

Perhaps you are feeling good about the progress you are making. You just need more time under your belt to be certain that the changes are going to last. That makes perfect sense. If that's true for you, you have a homework assignment. Simply continue to pay attention to what you and your spouse are doing that is working. Every time you feel at peace, joy, happy, connected or loving, notice what is going on around you. Keep track of your solutions.

Toward this end, you might consider keeping a solution journal. Noticing things you both are doing that contribute to a sense of well-being will offer you a formula for feeling joy in your marriage. Become a solution detective. Emphasize things that move you both in a positive direction. Again, what you focus on expands.

CHAPTER SIX

MORE TASKS FOR THE UNFAITHFUL SPOUSE

A S I TOLD your spouse in the last chapter, you deserve kudos for your determination to work through this challenging time in your life. I know this hasn't been easy and there have probably been days when you've asked yourself if your marriage was going to make it; but here you are, plowing through obstacles in order to make your relationship better than ever. Good for you.

Even if your marriage is now considerably better than the early days of this healing journey, I'm guessing you probably haven't received frequent positive feedback about your efforts. Your spouse was probably hurting too much to pat you on the back for all that you've been doing. I just want you to know that if your life together is better, it wouldn't have happened without a sincere, gargantuan effort on your part. So, you should feel good about yourself and your commitment to being a person of integrity no matter what. Take some time to appreciate this about yourself.

It's time to move into the next phase of healing: rebuilding.

Although there are some differences in what you and your spouse will need to do in this phase, there are also overlapping tasks. For that reason, I'd like you to make sure you read the last chapter just before this one because much of it applies to you and I don't want to repeat myself here. Although you're just about to read a section on goal-setting, what I wrote about establishing goals in the last chapter is a bit different and will also be helpful information for you to know. Also, the section on Love Languages in the previous chapter is a not-to-be-missed topic. Learning how to communicate your love so that it is received by your partner will make all the difference in the world. So, if you haven't done so already, read Chapter 5 before proceeding! Okay, I'll stop nagging.

Identify what needs to change in your marriage

It is time to get clear about exactly how you want your marriage to change or improve. When I say that to someone who has been unfaithful, they usually have one of several reactions.

Some people are extremely relieved to have the opportunity to express what has been missing in their relationship. They want to share what has been in their hearts, what they've been longing for. Frequently, they haven't been completely open and honest about their emotional void because they were afraid of hurting their spouses. But the route they chose- to have an affair- ended up hurting their spouses much more than it would have if only they'd been brutally, but lovingly, honest.

Other people have been honest in their marriages, but when their requests fell on deaf ears, they backed down and suffered in silence. They told themselves, "I tried everything. But it was all in vain." Feeling deflated, they withdrew emotionally.

When I work with folks who tried unsuccessfully to get their needs known and met, I have to be honest: it is clear to me that many gave up trying to get their partner to hear them, much too easily. When there is a big emotional void in a marriage, the person yearning for more must dig in with all they have, and stand their ground about their "bottom line needs" rather than resorting to giving up, letting things slide, allowing their inner emptiness to take hold. Usually their unhappiness is justifiable and their unmet needs are worth fighting for. But if a person doesn't feel they deserve to have their needs met in a marriage or isn't accustomed to standing their ground when something vital is missing, they may not have the tools to know how to proceed.

Many people acquiesce because they can't stand conflict. Often, these people grew up in families where there was a great deal of yelling, screaming and fighting. As a result, when they marry, these people vow to avoid conflict at all costs. The word is mum.

Other times, people grew up in families where they saw absolutely no conflict. To them, fighting, debating or even strong disagreements is off-limits; they're just not used to the tension, preferring to sweep things under the carpet and go on pretending all is well.

Either way, it's not a good idea to have a private, burning desire for things to be different in your marriage, and not be willing to force a crisis, and go to the mat over it. William Shakespeare once wrote, "Give sorrow words; the grief that does not speak knits up the o'er wrought heart and bids it break."

Do you recognize yourself in either of these descriptions? If so, this section will help you get specific about the changes you'd like to see in your marriage and offer you ways to communicate to your spouse.

In addition to being conflict avoidant, there are other reasons people don't openly express what they need from their spouses. Some people feel so much guilt and remorse about having strayed, they don't feel entitled to ask for anything for themselves. They feel relieved that their partners are willing to stay in the marriage after such a significant transgression, and don't want to burden them with any other requests.

If you can identify with not wanting to add to your spouse's burden by being honest about what was (or is) missing in your marriage, let me help you rethink this stance. If the issues in your marriage don't get addressed openly and honestly, you might very well find yourself in a similar situation in the future. If you have some concerns about your relationship, now's the time to tackle them. You deserve to enjoy your life. And when you're happier, your spouse will be happier too.

Finally, some people aren't inclined to set new marriage goals because they tell me their marriages are fine; they're happy with things just as they are. While research has shown that some unfaithful people truly have no complaints about their spouses, the fact remains, (as I said earlier in this book), that problems have certainly surfaced since the infidelity was acknowledged. Having affairs, and finding out about them, undermines the foundation of trust in marriage, which requires hard work to rebuild.

So, even if you felt good about your marriage prior to having an affair, there is work to be done now. And you both have to identify and voice those concerns.

Ask yourself, "How would I like my marriage to change or improve?" This could be a change in how the two of you interact, or it could mean you'd like for your spouse to do something differently. Really think about this. And while you're thinking about it, make sure your response is stated in action-oriented terms. You probably know what I mean by now, but since I want to be certain of that, I will give you an example.

Instead of saying, "I want my wife to be more sexual," say, "I would like to have sex at least twice a week and have her initiate it more often." Instead of saying, "I would really like us to have better communication," say, "I would love it if we would talk about how our days went sometime in the evenings. I would also like to discuss more personal issues such as our feelings rather than having kid-oriented conversations." Finally, instead of saying, "I would like more respect," say, "I would really appreciate it if you backed me up when it comes to dealing with the kids."

So, your first step is to describe your goal in action-oriented terms.

Next, please make sure that you are asking for what you'd like in the future as opposed to complaining about what's happened in the past. For instance, instead of saying, "I can't stand your sloppiness," say, "I would really like it if you would clean up the piles around the house." Or, instead of saying, "I wish you hadn't gained all that weight," say, "It would mean a lot to me if you would take better care of yourself and get into shape again."

One more example. Rather than saying, "I dislike that you still don't trust me," say, "It would be great if you would have some faith in me and point out what I've been doing right in my efforts to win back your trust." Get it?

In fact, you and your spouse should consider writing down your goals and sharing your thoughts with each other. Seeing your dreams printed in black and white often makes them materialize more readily.

Promise to commit to the changes you've made

You know the saying, "Actions speak louder than words?" Well, that's true. Still, for many people, words have a very powerful impact as well. And if you happen to be married to a person who puts a great deal of emphasis on words, it's essential that you not only change your behavior (a given) but that you *tell* your spouse you intend to be "the new you" both now, and in the future. You need to *say,* "I will make working on myself and our marriage a way of life. I'm not just going through the motions to avoid marital disaster. I want to do whatever it takes to make our marriage happy and strong for the long haul."

You can tell your spouse about your commitment in a heartfelt conversation, or you can write a letter, email or a give him or her a card. Do whatever you believe will mean the most to your spouse based on prior experiences. If a Hallmark card really touched your mate's heart in the past, do that again. If an open-hearted, genuine letter melted the ice years ago, it might be a good bet now. Just make sure you promise to make your marriage a major priority and that you will not take anything for granted.

At the risk of repeating myself here, let me say it again. Now that you've been doing the hard work of winning back your spouse's heart through your actions, don't forget to *talk* about your intentions to stay the course. This is especially true if you're married to someone who is verbally-oriented. Words will soothe your partner's soul.

Identify your triggers

For a variety for reasons, even with the best of intentions, it's possible to find yourself feeling tempted to engage in unhealthy behaviors that could hurt you or your marriage in the long run. Since you're committed to being faithful, it helps to take a closer look at the situations that could trip you up, and lead you down a path to disaster. You want to either avoid these situations or have a solid game plan for dealing with them should they arise.

First, it is important to understand that having thoughts about sex, or feeling attracted to people other than your spouse is natural. Don't judge yourself when that happens. Keep in mind, though, that *thinking* sexy thoughts is completely different from *acting* on them. If you truly intend to move forward in your marriage, you need to be able to make good choices, choices that will further your healing journey. You need to make choices that are not impulsive, but thoughtful and clear.

In order to make good choices, it helps to have a plan. You need to know what you will and won't do to honor your commitments and protect your marriage. Start by examining the times, places and people in your life that played a part in your decision to have an affair. These factors could very well be triggers for you, situations that could tempt you to behave in destructive ways.

So ask yourself, "Do I have certain friends who've been a bad influence on me?" Perhaps you have single friends who like to party and have encouraged you to do the same. It's important to spend time around people who value your goals for your marriage. You might have to be direct with old friends as you tell them you have new goals to prioritize your marriage and honor your marital vows. How will you handle it if someone chides you about not being the life of the party anymore or being less sociable? What, exactly, will you say if they challenge you?

Or perhaps your affair partner continues to show up in various places in your life and tempts you to continue the relationship. Think about where this is most likely to happen, and how you will respond if you see them walking toward you in a gym, or grocery store, or anywhere you are likely to run into them. Will you walk the other way? Will you say something? If you say something, how can you say it in a way that will get the message across that your relationship is truly over? You might have an imaginary role play in your mind. Have a concrete plan.

Are there certain situations that lend themselves to "dangerous liaisons," such as going to bars, clubs or other social gatherings where other people might be interested in finding sexual partners? Are there activities at work that might put you in contact with people who don't respect your new boundaries? Do you have hobbies that could be threatening to your marriage?

When in conversation with strangers, do you find yourself "acting single" and intentionally avoiding discussing your marital status? (Did you avoid wearing your wedding ring in certain situations?) Have you told yourself that having friends of the opposite sex is reasonable, but looking back on it, do you realize that many of these friends eventually became lovers?

Think about how your affair happened. Were there too many late night meetings at work? Did occasional lunch plans morph into regular dinner dates with a co-worker? Was alcohol often a part of the interaction? Have frequent intimate conversations been a precursor to wanting physical connection?

Be honest with yourself about situations that will require great will power to stay the course. Again, whenever possible, redesign your life so that you can avoid these situations. Think about the changes you need to make so that you feel good about your upright and honest choices. Let me give you an example.

I was working with a man who had had several affairs but desperately wanted to stop that behavior and save his marriage. He was a highly esteemed photographer who often attended gallery events that showcased his work. Many women would admire his photographs and want to speak with him about his craft. Often the conversations became too personal and he would find himself flirting with his "fans."

In talking with him about triggers, he said, "I see it like this. I need to think about my actions in terms of green, yellow and red lights. Green lights are behaviors that are good for me and my marriage. Yellow lights are questionable behaviors; they're too risky. Red lights are behaviors I have to stop. I shouldn't be engaging in those interactions at all."

Then I asked him to tell me a little more about what kinds of behaviors constituted each category. Here's what he said:

"I am too physical with women. I hug them and that's not ok. Unless it's my wife or a dear friend of both of ours, hugging is a red light behavior. Also, women ask me about my work. Answering them politely is green light behavior. But going into lengthy, in-depth personal discussions about my art, is how I flirt with women and that needs to become a red light category immediately."

He went on to say, "I used to go to these events with my wife, but when we were there, we would split up and socialize in opposite corners of the room. Now I know that, although splitting up might be a yellow light behavior, I have to make sure I check in with my wife regularly so that everyone feels her presence there. That includes the women interested in my photos."

You get the picture? Some behaviors are marriage-friendly and others simply are not. Get clear about what will keep you on track and promise yourself you will avoid unnecessary temptation.

Describe in detail your expectations about monogamy

When you decided to have an affair, chances are, you broke a spoken or unspoken vow you made with your spouse. Moving forward, it will be important for you both to be clear about your expectations regarding monogamy and what constitutes betrayal.

Will you have sex only with each other? What about having friends of the opposite sex? If opposite sex friends are agreeable, can you have dinner together, spend weekends together doing hobbies?

Is it acceptable to have deeply emotional relationships with other people of the opposite sex that don't include your spouse? What about texting? What about private Facebook or email accounts? Is it okay to have weekends away with single buddies? What about the use of porn?

Since you are designing your future relationship, there are many questions you and your spouse need to sort out. I recommend an excellent book to help guide you both in the process of identifying your expectations regarding your marriage. It's called, THE NEW MONOGAMY, by Tammy Nelson, Ph.D. She offers lists of excellent questions to ask yourself and each other about what will make your marriage feel both alive *and* safe. Unless you pinpoint exactly how each of you feels about various topics, you might find yourselves experiencing disappointment and betrayal once again.

After deciding what your new marriage will look like moving forward, Dr. Nelson suggests that you write down and finalize your agreements. Furthermore, she suggests you make it official by dating, signing and keeping your agreement in a safe place. She believes you should both have a copy that you should revisit regularly as a point of discussion. This will ensure that you remain in agreement about your vision for the future.

Deal with your residual grief

In an earlier chapter, I told you that you might feel sadness about ending your affair, even if breaking it off is something you wanted and needed to do. If the relationship was meaningful to you in any way, ending it can create a sense of longing, even grief, if you thought you loved them. You might even feel some resentment about having to make the choice to terminate that relationship.

As I said before, feeling grief when there is a loss is completely normal. If you have had feelings of sadness, I know this has been hard for you because it's probably not something you feel free to talk about with your spouse. You might have kept these feelings to yourself or you've talked to trusted friends or relatives.

Still, you might be wondering if something is wrong with you or your marriage if you find yourself thinking, even day dreaming about your affair partner. I want you to know that, even if weeks or months have passed and your affair partner is on your mind, you should not be concerned or question your decision to work on your marriage. Allow the feelings of grief or sadness to be there. They're natural. Accept them.

A woman once wrote a letter telling me that though she had given up an affair five years earlier, she still found herself reminiscing about that relationship. She wondered if she should have continued the affair, and left her marriage. She questioned whether her lingering thoughts about the affair meant that she had made a mistake.

I wrote her back telling her that her feelings were completely normal and that her memories and feelings about the relationship were hers to have and hold. I told her that she could always honor the relationship in her mind and in her heart, and that no one could take that away from her. I suggested that she stop trying to rid herself of the feelings and just accept her thoughts as they arose in her mind.

She wrote me back to tell me that she thought the suggestion was brilliant, that no one had ever told her to just accept what is. The harder she tried to rid herself of her feelings, the more pronounced they became.

Now, because she no longer judged herself for having thoughts or feelings about the affair, the memories started to fade a bit and settle comfortably into the background. She was very grateful for the suggestion.

I am making this same suggestion to you. Grief has its own time line. It doesn't end simply because you think it should. Grief is a process. You should trust the process. You will get to the other side.

If, after trying to put my suggestion to use, you are still struggling with your feelings, it might be a good idea for you to talk to a therapist who can help you work through lingering emotions.

Forgive yourself

After infidelity has happened in a marriage, when people think about forgiveness, most people immediately think that the betrayed spouse must forgive the unfaithful spouse. It certainly helps when that happens.

But something equally important has to take place. If you've been hard on yourself for choosing to have an affair and lying to your spouse about it, there comes a time when you have to forgive yourself. You are not a bad person. You are a good person who made a choice that ultimately hurt your spouse and your marriage. But you are trying to find your way. You have been working hard on yourself and also working hard to rebuild your marriage. You care deeply about your spouse's feelings.

I'm sure if you did an inventory of your life, you could acknowledge many things you have done right. You would see the contributions you have made to your marriage and your family. You never meant to hurt anyone. In fact, hurting your spouse was probably the last thing you ever wanted to do. It's time to focus on what's good about you and your actions and let go of all the judgment and self-recrimination. It doesn't serve you. For that matter, it doesn't serve anyone. As I told you before, the more guilt and shame you feel, the less present you can be for others, especially your spouse.

Look, everyone makes mistakes; no one is perfect. There are many reasons you might have strayed. I believe if you become unhappy in the months and years ahead, you will find more productive ways of creating change in your life and in your marriage. Let the past be in the past. Start tomorrow with a clean slate. Be kind to yourself. Forgive yourself. You deserve it. Maya Angelou once said, "It's one of the greatest gifts you can give yourself, to forgive. Forgive everybody." That includes you.

CHAPTER SEVEN

BECOMING SEXUAL AGAIN

COUPLES DEALING WITH infidelity often wonder, "*When is the right time to become sexual again?*" Some couples have sex very soon after the discovery of an affair. And many say that it is incredibly hot, passionate sex. Occasionally, they even tell me that it is the best sex they've ever had. Others feel so hurt and betrayed that they can't imagine ever being sexual with their spouses again. And then there's everyone in between.

The truth is, there is no single answer to the question, "When should couples resume their sexual relationships after infidelity?" Everyone is different and these differences must be honored and respected.

If you are someone who chose to be physically intimate with your spouse shortly after finding out about an affair, it is important for you to know that this is perfectly normal. I say this because many people express embarrassment and shame about their decision to become sexual with their unfaithful spouses. This is unfortunate.

Healing takes many paths. Some people need to experience "make-up sex." They feel that touching creates more closeness than words ever can. For many couples, make-up sex has been part of shared marital history. Reconnecting after fights by being sexually intimate has worked for them. Everything seems right in the world after making love. Plus, driven by a strong need to not feel separate; the need to hug, kiss, fondle, caress and make love makes perfect sense.

Believe it or not, many couples tell me that they are not only having hot sex immediately following the discovery of infidelity, but that their sexual relationship continues to improve long after this initial period as well. This is particularly true if their sex lives were on the back burner prior to the infidelity. After the affair, they stopped taking each other for granted. They put a great deal of energy into staying physically connected to each other.

If you and your spouse fit this description, you probably don't need much help right now to rebuild your sexual relationship. You've found your way back to each other. You just need to make sure that your passion and desire continues. Whatever you've been doing over the past weeks or months should become a way of life.

So examine what you've been doing that has been helpful. Have you set aside more time for intimacy? Have you been doing more talking about your sexual needs? Have you told the kids that you require private time? Are you being more adventurous and passionate when you're having sex? What seems to be working for you? That's what you need to continue to do over time. Make a commitment to be intentional about preserving what's been going well.

On the other hand, your sex life might be suffering because of the infidelity. You may be dreading sexually intimacy with your mate because you feel devastated that your spouse was sexual with someone else. Or you might want sex, but each time you begin to touch your spouse, you become flooded with a barrage of intense emotions. Maybe the thought of having sex brings to mind images of the affair partner which stops you dead in your tracks.

Or perhaps because you had the affair, you still feel guilty, and being intimate with your spouse makes you feel even worse. It's also possible that, because you feel uncertain if your spouse wants to have sex, you're cautious; you simply don't approach them. Maybe your spouse cried or got very angry suddenly when you were in the middle of trying to rekindle your sexual connection. You might feel overwhelmed by their emotions and simply not know what to do anymore.

If your sex life is not where you want it to be yet, I will offer you help in this chapter. Having a good sexual relationship, one that is satisfying to both of you, is important for your marital well-being. Touching raises oxytocin levels in our blood which affects the neurotransmitters in our brain and stimulates feelings of closeness, relaxation and pleasure. In fact, oxytocin is considered the bonding hormone. We feel connected to people when oxytocin is flowing. Nursing mothers have increased levels of oxytocin. Having sex and achieving orgasms increases oxytocin. It's also called the love hormone. Without touch, people feel distant and separate from one another.

If your sexual relationship has never been good, there's no time like the present to change that. This crisis in your marriage has given you opportunities to really look under the hood and decide how you want your relationship to be and what needs to change to get it to a better place. You may realize that you want professional help with this. I will give you information about working with a sex therapist later in this chapter. But, in the meantime, you can start working on a few things yourselves.

First of all, it's important to realize that, if you've been hesitant for any reason to become sexual again, you may have to nudge yourself a bit at first. You have to *decide* that being physically intimate is important. Then, recognize that intense feelings of desire may not just happen spontaneously; you might have to be proactive to help make them happen.

Just for the record, I'm not suggesting that you can just will yourself to feel desire; but I am suggesting that you can take steps that will make desire a more likely outcome. You can create the conditions that often trigger more passionate feelings and responses within.

At this juncture in your healing process, I'm assuming that the two of you have done a great deal of work on your marriage and you're feeling that your relationship is considerably more stable than it was a few weeks or months ago. Conventional wisdom suggests that if things are going better emotionally, this will automatically lead to a better physical relationship. Conventional wisdom isn't always right. Sometimes, people feel quite close emotionally but it doesn't necessarily translate into a more active and satisfying sex life. Don't expect your hesitant feelings to just miraculously change, out of the blue, one day. Without a concerted effort, they likely won't.

Start by talking to each other about your feelings about your sex life and how you each feel about it. Talk about where you're at right now, but more importantly, discuss where you'd like things to be. Be concrete. What would make you feel a little more like being close physically? Would you like to start by being able to touch in affectionate ways without the expectation that sex will follow? Would you enjoy cuddling or backrubs, but simply aren't quite ready for sex? It may be easier to start out with affectionate touch and work your way to being more sexual later.

What kind of touch feels okay to you right now? Does a hug or kiss feel safe? Is it okay to hold hands, or maybe give and receive a foot rub? Does a short embrace feel good but not a lingering one? It's time to get clear about what feels good and right and share your thoughts with your partner.

It's amazing to me how many couples who have been married for long periods of time rarely, if ever, talk about sex. It's been a taboo subject. This is extremely unfortunate because no one is a mind reader. Unless you speak up, your spouse won't know what pleases you, what turns you on.

Often, in the beginning of relationships, couples shared their sexual interests, dreams, passions and needs. But once they shared their thoughts early on, they think their job is done. They think they know all they need to know about their spouse's sexuality. But this is where faulty thinking comes in. Because what turns people on early in their relationships is often different from what turns them on later on in life. Our bodies change. What we need from each other in order to feel aroused also changes. If we don't have on-going, transparent conversations with each other, there's no way we can really know what's in our spouse's mind and heart about being physically connected and satisfied.

I'd like to share an example of a conversation I had with a couple in my practice who had been married for 25 years. They were trying to revive their physical relationship after the discovery of infidelity. I was encouraging them to talk about ways to feel affectionate in order to break the ice and take steps toward intimacy again. Listen in:

Michele: It may be early in the process, but I think it may be good to talk about ways that you can be physically intimate with each other that don't involve intercourse. Can you talk about that a little bit?

Steve: Well, she is the best hugger on the planet, so it's not that she's not approachable. But early morning is probably not going to happen for an hour or an hour and a half until after we wake up.

Helen: That's not accurate.

Steve: OK, but I guess that what I'm saying is that for me, I would enjoy that. On the other hand, I enjoy holding my wife and I'd like to be able to touch her again intimately and have her touch me. We kind of need to work our way back into it. We gotta get our "mojo" back. I admit that I have fear about approaching her and not really turning her on enough so that she would want to have more than just the foreplay.

Michele: Have you talked about that?

Steve: No, we haven't talked about it at all.

Michele: (To Helen) What do you think when he says that he is kind of nervous about not being able to satisfy you?

Helen: (long pause)…Selfishly, I'm thinking that he *should* be nervous because he doesn't listen to me when I tell him what I do enjoy.

Michele: What is it that you want him to know?

Helen: I just want him to open his ears when I tell him what satisfies me.

Michele: Like?

Helen: When you approach me, it's generally in a good old junior high school boy's way- grab the ass first, ask questions later. How about a, "How are you doing, are you busy right now, is this a good time?" I'm a female and I just don't like the grab an ass first. Come and hug me first.

Run your hand down my body and then hit the gas. Don't just go for the obvious things that you want to touch first. It starts my engine and makes me more interested.

When you kiss me, don't kiss me with an open mouth with your tongue sticking out. Kiss me on the lips first. And then work into the French kiss. That makes me want to French kiss. That makes me want to have your hands on me more. The approach of just like – (she gestures grabbing her breasts) is just off putting to me. (He listens attentively and looks at her the whole time she is speaking.)

If you could just slow it down to a slower gear and then work your way through the gears instead of…what would my Camaro do if you started it in 6th gear?

Steve: (Laughs) It wouldn't be happy.

Helen: It would be screaming like me. I am not unapproachable, it's worth your time to slow things down to first gear and work your way through the gears. It is, I promise.

You said that I'm not good in the morning. You don't know that. But one thing that will wake me up in the morning is somebody running his hands down my body, sneaking up behind me and spooning me and giving me a hug. Best way in the whole world to wake me up. Twenty five years and you don't know that about me.

This conversation illustrates how important it is to talk about your turn-on buttons and to be specific. The only tweaking I would do in the above conversation is to tell you that it helps to talk about what you *like* rather than delve into details regarding what you are *unhappy* about. But be *specific* about your preferences. It will make all the difference.

If talking is challenging, you can use non-verbal methods of helping your spouse learn your sexual needs. A well-timed moan, meaningful glance, satisfied smile, or a guided hand are powerful ways to communicate pleasure.

If you haven't been sexual for a while and it feels awkward and uncomfortable to get going, you can consider starting with some exercises many sex therapists use as they start working with couples. They're called Sensate Focus exercises.

Sensate Focus exercises were originally developed by Masters and Johnson. The goal of these exercises is to become more aware of the sensations that are pleasurable and those that are not pleasurable rather than simply focusing on having an orgasm. It takes the pressure out of being "goal-oriented" and helps people relax.

Sensate Focus exercises encourage spouses to explore their partners' bodies slowly and get feedback about what feels good and what doesn't. Done properly, these exercises can strengthen relationships and improve communication skills. Although there is some variety in how these exercises are done, I'll give you a brief example so you can see if this method of jump-starting intimacy is one that you'd both like to pursue further.

Before you begin these exercises, you might consider setting the stage for a relaxing, enjoyable experience. Think about what you might find to be soothing and calming. You might start by taking a warm bath and turning the lights down low. You might turn on some relaxing background music that you love. How about lighting candles or incense? Anything that sets the tone for a pleasant interaction will add to the experience.

In Stage 1 of these exercises, couples take turns touching each other's bodies. The "toucher" focuses on what it *feels* like to touch his or her partner rather than trying to figure out what might please him or her. The "receiver" should focus on being in the moment, paying attention to the sensations that arise when being touched. It is permissible to voice pleasure or ask that touch be given in a different way. But other than that, there should be no speaking during the exercise. Additionally, during Stage 1, genitals are strictly off-limits. Sexual intercourse is not permitted during this stage.

The second stage includes touching of breasts but not genitals. During this stage, it is permissible to guide your partner's hand to offer feedback about what feels good in terms of pressure or pace. Intercourse is still not permissible. Couples should stay focused on learning about their own and each other's bodies and what feels pleasurable and sensual.

Stage 3 introduces genitals and intercourse. Again, the emphasis is on touch, sensation, feelings, but not orgasm. These exercises are relaxing, pleasurable and therapeutic. You can learn about your bodies in new, comfortable ways. You can take your time getting to know each other again.

If easing into a sexual relationship sounds appealing to you, there are many resources online, in self-help books and in sex therapy. If you'd like more information about Sensate Focus exercises, simply Google the term. You'll have no trouble finding good information about this. If you decide you'd like to work with a sex therapist, I suggest you seek help from a therapist who specializes in sex therapy and is licensed. You can find a directory of licensed sex therapists on the website for the American Association of Sexuality Educators, Counselors and Therapists.

What if your heart is in the right place, but being physically close is too challenging or threatening right now? Perhaps every time you are sexual with your spouse, you feel triggered. You start thinking about the affair partner. You might be thinking, "Is she more attractive or a better lover than me?" "Did you love him more than me?" "If you loved her, how is our relationship different or special?" "Did she have bigger breasts than me?" "Did he have a bigger penis?" And so on. If this happens, what should you do? There are several options.

First, simply allow your thoughts and feelings to be what they are. Take a break from being sexual at the moment. Talk about what's happening inside your head. Discuss your pain together. Don't blame or point fingers. Just talk about what you're feeling openly. Don't be afraid to cry. Cry together. Pull together. Be teammates.

If you're the partner who had the affair, be emotionally available. Express regret, remorse, sadness. Be empathetic. Ask if there's anything you can do to help your spouse through this rough patch. A good question to ask is, "What can I say or do that might feel soothing to you right now? Because I want to comfort you and reassure you, but I'm not sure what helps you the most." Tell your spouse that you understand how hard this must be for them. Reassure them by saying that you are going to be there no matter how long it takes; you're not going anywhere.

Embrace. Breathe. Be together.

Sometimes you can resume touching each other after you've talked. Other times, it's best to stop what you're doing and come back to touching at another time. Be patient with these starts and stops. Know that there will be a day when run-away emotions stop taking on a life of their own. How calmly you handle these difficult times will make a big difference in how quickly you can move beyond them.

If talking about your feelings with each other doesn't seem to help, there is another viable option in terms of how to handle intrusive emotions, the kind of emotions that sabotage your ability to feel close and sexual. *Don't* talk about them. Instead, re-read what

I wrote in Chapter 5 about the technique of thought-stopping. You will recall that thought-stopping is a method for changing your mental channel when you're having thoughts or images that aren't helpful to your ultimate goals of feeling better and becoming closer. Thought-stopping enables you to take a deep breath, and refocus. It helps you remain present.

What does it mean if you continue to find yourself ruminating about the affair and it's getting in the way of emotional closeness and physical intimacy? It probably means one of two things.

The spouse who betrayed the marriage might not be doing their work. He or she might not be reassuring, empathetic or remorseful enough. It's hard to resume a physical relationship if you're not feeling close to your spouse because they haven't been fully committed to doing the program outlined in this book. If you believe this is so, you need to identify what you'd like your spouse to do differently so you feel you're on the same team. You need to feel safe in your marriage to move forward. If you don't, figure out what's preventing that and talk about it. Ask for what you need.

On the other hand, perhaps your spouse *has* been faithful and is working hard to win back your trust and your love. It's possible that you haven't been giving your spouse the credit they truly deserve. Your spouse may have accused you of punishing him or her by withholding sex. While punishment might not be your intention, it is helpful to understand that the result of your actions may still *feel* like punishment to your mate.

Some people who are hesitant to become sexual again will tell me something like this, I'm afraid if I yield to having sex with him too quickly, he'll think I've forgotten about the affair and everything is back the way it was, perfectly okay."

Believe me, your spouse knows you haven't forgotten about the affair! As I told you before, you will never forget the affair, nor should you. You both need to remember how you got here and focus on what you need to do to avoid ever being here again.

And speaking of this, projecting worries into the future, and wondering if your spouse will betray you again will short-circuit progress. If you find you are constantly worrying about the next possible betrayal, it's likely that this loop has been at the root of why you're not moving forward. Worrying about your spouse's intentions and actions in the future has probably stood in the way of your relaxing and feeling pleasure when you're being touched and caressed. You don't want to be hurt again.

I understand this completely! Who wouldn't? But you have to do an honest inventory of the steps your partner has taken to try to make your marriage work. Has your spouse been diligent about trying to help you feel better and working hard to rebuild trust? If your answer is a resounding, "Yes," then I'm encouraging you to push yourself and risk loving again. You wouldn't be reading this book if love and connection weren't important to you. You wouldn't have gotten this far if you didn't have dreams of putting this pain behind you. You can do this. You can choose love. And once you do, you will feel safe in each other's embrace.

There's one more point I'd like to add for those who have felt the sting of betrayal and who are wondering if they'll ever feel safe and secure in the future. The key in really feeling safe is to do enough work on *yourself*, to feel good about who you are, to know that you're a great person in spite of what has happened. If you love yourself, you will know that you will be fine in the future no matter what your spouse does or doesn't do. Your sense of security will come from within. You will realize that, regardless of what happens in the future, you will land on your feet. You've got to get to this point in your own journey to feel centered. Your spouse can certainly help you enormously, but in the end, you need to know that you will be okay no matter what. You are okay. You're way more than okay, in fact. Remind yourself of this regularly. It will be easier to let your guard down when you fully appreciate that your personal stability and well-being ultimately rest in your hands.

What if you're the spouse who was unfaithful and you have been timid about initiating sex because you aren't sure that your partner is interested? Again, the best thing to do is to talk about it. Tell your spouse you're longing to be close physically and you're confused about the best way to proceed. If you feel like you've been getting mixed signals, describe what you've observed and ask for clarification. You might say, "You know, last night you seemed to be enjoying the evening and I really wanted to kiss you. I wasn't sure if that would've been okay with you. I don't want you to feel pressured, so I didn't reach out to you. But I'd like to know if you'd be open to my kissing or hugging you. I'd really like to do that. Are you okay with that?"

The other option is to just take a risk and touch your spouse lovingly. See what happens. Your spouse might be very receptive. If not, you'll know and you can pull back. But it's important to ask, "What can I do that will help you feel like _____(kissing, touching, having sex)?" It may just be a matter of time. You may both just have to be a bit more patient.

If you are reluctant to re-engage sexually, here's another possible cause to consider. Is it possible that, aside from the fallout of the affair, you have always been the partner who is less interested in physical contact? Have the two of you had a sexual desire gap long before the infidelity ever took place?

If this is the case, you might be in a sex-starved marriage. A sex-starved marriage isn't necessarily a relationship with no sex. A sex-starved marriage occurs when one spouse is desperately longing for more touch and the other spouse isn't "into it" and doesn't understand its appeal. The lower desire spouse often thinks, "It's just sex, what's the big deal?"

But to the spouse yearning for touch, it's a very big deal because it's about feeling wanted, loved, connected emotionally and treasured in the relationship. And when this disconnect happens, what also happens is that emotional intimacy suffers; couples stop sitting on the couch together, they stop laughing at each other's jokes, they stop spending time together and being friends. And it places the marriage at risk for infidelity and divorce.

Have you heard the adage, "he who cares least has the most power?" Although it's rarely admitted, when there is a sexual desire gap, the person with lower desire controls the sexual relationship. This is not to say that the less interested person is controlling the relationship intentionally or in a mean-spirited way; it just means that if the low desire spouse doesn't want to have sex, sex probably isn't going to happen.

As a result, the higher desire spouse feels enormous rejection. It breaks their heart. I've seen countless people cry as they've shared the intense pain they've felt over repeated rejections. In fact, feeling rejected is one of the most painful of all human emotions. The problem is, when higher desire spouses feel rejected, eventually they go from feeling inwardly hurt to turning outwardly angry. Anger pushes the lower desire spouse even further away and leaves them feeling justified and resentful. Intimacy becomes less and less likely.

So, what can be done about this sexual divide? For starters, if this sounds familiar to you, I strongly recommend that you read my book, THE SEX-STARVED MARRIAGE. It will definitely help you navigate your way to a solution. And while you're at it, you and your spouse should listen to my TEDx talk on the same topic. It will be a great jumping off point to begin a frank discussion on the topic.

But here's something you can do right away. If you are the person who has had lower sex drive in your relationship, part of the reason you haven't been all that interested in being sexual now is because sex has never been one of your top desires or priorities. Yes, unquestionably, there are different issues at play now that there has been an affair in your history, but you need to take a look at the past. Honestly ask yourself if sex has been a low priority to you.

If, in your quiet moments, you understand what I'm saying here, it's time to take a closer look at what you need to do differently. You need to make your sexual relationship a bigger priority in your life. "How can I do this if I'm not in the mood" you may ask. Good question. Here's the answer.

Have you ever experienced not being in the mood when your spouse approached you for sex, but once you both got going and you lost yourself in the process, it felt good? You had an orgasm. You felt closer to your spouse. Do you identify with what I'm saying here?

I've had countless people, albeit mostly women, who have said that they often aren't thinking about sex or in the mood for sex; but if they just accept their husbands' advances and relax, sex is great.

There's actually some science to this. Research shows that 50% of the population has to be physically stimulated or aroused before they actually realize they have sexual desire. They don't have spontaneous sexual thoughts. Desire follows arousal rather than the other way around. It's not that desire is absent; it's just that touching must come before the brain signals, "This is fun." Ironically, most of these people are married to partners who have random lusty thoughts on a regular basis. It's just that everyone is wired differently. Some people think about sex all the time, others never do. But it doesn't mean that those in the "never-do" group don't enjoy sex once they're into it!

The solution? If you rarely fantasize about sex, then I suggest you adopt the Nike philosophy and "Just Do It." It's important to allow yourself to be receptive to your partner's advances even from a neutral place. You don't have to feel fireworks or great longing for sex to get started, you just have to be receptive. Your body will take over from there.

If, however, you haven't enjoyed sex in the past and you're not particularly interested in it now, you need to find out why. It's possible that you've had a troubled past- sexual abuse, emotional abuse- or that you feel pain during intercourse. It's also possible that sex hasn't been enjoyable because your partner doesn't know how to satisfy you. Or, you may have gotten bad messages about sex when you were young. Perhaps you've never had an orgasm. Or perhaps your hormones are out of balance. If this is so, adopting the Nike philosophy may be an over-simplification for you. You may need some help sorting through these issues. I strongly recommend that you seek professional advice to help you discover the pleasure that comes from being connected both emotionally and sexually to your partner.

Before you get the wrong idea and think that only women have lower desire, I can tell you, this simply isn't true. Men have low sexual desire too. They just don't talk about it very much. And as a result, many higher desire women suffer in silence. If you're a man whose sexual desire is lower than your wife's, then you, too, need to know that it's time to repair your sexual relationship. I also wrote a book entitled, THE SEX-STARVED WIFE. This book will help both of you as well.

In short, whether you're a man or a woman who hasn't been into sex, I'm suggesting that it's imperative that you not be complacent about your sexual relationship. We know so much now about how to help people increase their sexual desire, at any age, and there is no reason that anyone who wants a more robust sex life can't have one. That includes you!

One final thought about getting sexy again. Sometimes it's not the *betrayed* spouse who puts up a wall when it comes to being sexual again; it's the unfaithful partner. Why is this so? If you are the unfaithful spouse, there might be many reasons you are hesitant to resume a physical relationship. One explanation is that you have lingering feelings and thoughts about your affair partner. If so, please re-read the section in Chapter 6 where I remind you that letting go of intense feelings often takes time and that it is completely normal to reminisce about the times you spent together with your affair partner. These thoughts will diminish over time. Stop judging yourself about this. The judgment, rather than your past actions, is what's keeping you apart from your spouse.

If your spouse is ready to be intimate with you again but you've been struggling to connect, read Chapter 5, a chapter for your spouse. In particular, read about the "thought-stopping" technique. It will help you stay focused on your marriage and remain present in the moment with your spouse. Every time your mind wanders and detracts from your sexual experience with your mate, remind yourself to come back to the room and feel the pleasurable sensations that are present when you allow yourself to focus on them.

Let's be frank: a mutually satisfying sexual relationship doesn't happen automatically, even when there *hasn't* been an affair. So, be patient and be pro-active. It takes a commitment, intention, time and energy to prioritize your sex life together again. (Or for the first time.) It helps to have a vision of where you'd like to be a few months from now. Allow yourselves to dream together about what will make your sexual relationship more erotic, playful, sensual, emotional, and satisfying. Talk about what would feel magical to each of you. What will make you feel really alive sexually? Be experimental. Cast your inhibitions to the wind. Imagine yourselves having the best sexual relationship ever. Ask yourself, "What will we be doing differently when we are enjoying wonderful sex on a regular basis?" And why not get some practice.....now?

PART IV

DOING IT ALONE

CHAPTER EIGHT

WHEN YOUR
SPOUSE WON'T END
THE AFFAIR

U P UNTIL NOW, I've assumed that you *and* your spouse have been working together to heal from infidelity. It is ideal when both partners are equally committed to working on their marriage. That said, life doesn't always work out the way you hope. In this chapter, I offer guidelines for what *you* can do to help piece your marriage back together if your spouse won't end the affair.

Sometimes, an unfaithful spouse doesn't feel remorse and regret about their actions. In fact, they may focus on the anger they feel about the way the affair was discovered ("How dare you spy on me!") or frustration over problems in the marriage. Little empathy is shown. And to make matters worse, they may not feel ready to end the affair.

If your spouse is unwilling to end the affair, they might be honest about their insistence on continuing the relationship.

On the other hand, they may simply continue to be deceitful as a way to avoid confrontation. If your spouse is deceitful- seeing the other person secretly and lying about it- you may feel tempted to spy, sneak around or constantly confront your partner. Let me share a number of reasons that becoming Sherlock Holmes isn't a good idea.

If your spouse isn't certain they want to stay in your marriage, then spying and confrontations will only make them feel angry, trapped, cornered and mistreated. Then guess who will receive all the blame for what's happening in your marriage? You. You'll be blamed for being so "suspicious" and "invading their privacy." This is a misguided, completely unfair argument. But if you are looking for results, I can tell you that it doesn't help to point out the error of their ways, or their lack of logic: it will fall on deaf ears.

If you really want to save your marriage, you have to be strategic, instead of naturally reactive, in how you approach your spouse. You need to back off for a while, as hard as that might seem. It might help to know that conventional wisdom suggests that most affairs eventually end. If you can allow time for the affair to unravel on its own without pressuring your spouse, there may soon come a time when they are ready to focus on the marriage again.

Your spouse probably felt infatuated with their affair partner. There's a lot of sheer adrenalin pumping when there is an illicit attraction. Everything is very exciting and titillating when it's new. Plus, your spouse doesn't have to deal with day to day issues with the person. Everything is romantic and fun.

But the good news is that infatuations tend to wear off. Newness fades. Their interactions, once so novel, become more routine. Frequently, people begin to realize that all relationships require work, even affairs. The bloom falls off the rose, as it were. It is during this time of "faded love," when many spouses begin to question themselves: "Am I really willing to lose my marriage and family to continue this affair?" The straying mate starts to consider the possibility that the pleasures derived from cheating aren't worth the costs. And that's when they come home emotionally.

As difficult and unfair is it may sound: most people have to come to the realization the consequences of leaving their marriage aren't worth the end result, *on their own*. They can't be convinced they shouldn't leave. In fact, trying to convince them often propels them further into rebellion: making them seek out the excitement of their lover's arms even more as a way to say, "You don't understand how deeply I feel for my affair partner. Plus, you can't control me."

So, if your spouse is determined to continue the affair, you have to stop trying to influence them to break it off. In my experience, I've seen that pressure to end an affair only forces an unfaithful spouse to dig in their heels even deeper. Or, it will encourage your spouse to continue seeing the affair partner but lie to you about it. I'm sure you've had enough lies to last a lifetime at this point. Don't do anything that will encourage your spouse to cover their tracks.

The deceit will make your spouse feel guilty. Guilt drives a wedge between spouses because your spouse will feel like avoiding you.

What can you do? Well, you can tell your spouse that you don't believe you can truly work on your marriage as long as they are seeing the other person. Say it clearly and matter-of-factly. Then, once you've stated it: *stop discussing it.* Your spouse already knows that it is impossible to move forward as long as there is an on-going affair. It's just that they aren't quite ready to focus completely on your marriage yet. So, state your expectations, but don't be repetitive.

The other thing you should refrain from doing is getting

friends and relatives to try to "talk sense" to your spouse. And don't contact the affair partner with pleas or threats. That will be seen as a form of control on your part and won't be received well. Far from it! Your spouse will use your "controlling behavior" as evidence that they really don't want to stay married. Don't give your spouse that out! Leave friends and family out of it.

And while I'm on the subject of leaving friends and family out of this, remember to re-read the section in Chapter 2 about the fallout of talking to well-meaning friends and family. When you tell them about the affair, they are likely to take sides with you, and encourage you to leave your marriage. If your goal is to save your marriage, only speak to people who will support your marriage despite the betrayal. Be careful about this!

I know it's a lot to ask of you to avoid putting pressure on your spouse to end the affair if your spouse has chosen unfaithfulness. You may feel like you're a doormat or that your spouse is "having his cake and eating it too." After all, your spouse has all the comforts of home- you, the kids (if you have them), your home and a secure life style- *and* an affair. How unfair this feels, and is. I get it.

But you are not a doormat. You are not a pushover. You are simply fighting for your marriage and you're trying to do it in the smartest way possible. You are giving your spouse the time and space they need to sort their emotions out and do the right thing. You are very courageous. You're a warrior. Don't let anyone tell you differently.

Perhaps you are thinking, "Michele, I hear you but I simply can't back off and say nothing when I know in my heart that my spouse is continuing the affair." You may feel like you must set limits. You might believe that, unless you draw a clear boundary about what you will or won't accept, you're not being true to yourself.

I understand that feeling completely. I might feel that way

myself. But if you proceed in setting a boundary or giving an ultimatum, you have to be prepared to follow through, which might mean ending your marriage.

Are you feeling compelled to draw a line in the sand? If so, are you also prepared to leave or to end your marriage? Don't make idle threats. Your spouse may call you on your bluff. And you need to be ready to call it quits.

It's possible that after working on your marriage for a long time without any help from your spouse, you may tire and feel that an ultimatum is exactly what is needed. And you may be right. But the key here is to allow the space for the affair to die a natural death before you take the risk of ending your marriage. So, go slowly. You can always get divorced, if you like. But once you go down that road, it's hard to turn back. Be wise. Take your time.

There's another advantage in taking your time. I've had some clients tell me, "Michele, I am so thankful I followed your advice for as long as I could. Even though, in the end, I was unable to save my marriage, I have peace that I turned over every rock I could, and that I didn't leave my marriage lightly or without concerted effort and taking wise advice and counsel. I allowed plenty of time for the ship to right itself. And I can look back and feel proud of myself about this." No matter what the end result for your marriage, taking things slowly is the prudent thing to do.

Since I told you to back off from pressuring your spouse for a while in order to give them space to sort out their emotions, I know I also need to offer advice about what you need to do *instead* of trying to convince your spouse to end the affair. It's hard to stop a behavior without replacing it with some other, more productive behavior.

Here's the scoop. You need to focus on yourself for a while. First of all, this means (sadly) that you can't expect your spouse to do the helpful things I've outlined in this book thus far, to help you feel better. It's not right, it's not fair, but it's a fact. Your spouse has very little to give you right now. But this doesn't mean that you have to walk around feeling miserable all the time. You need to find ways to self-soothe. Focus on things you can do to nurture yourself. Start by reviewing the section in Chapter 5 about the importance of finding ways to calm yourself and rebuild your self-esteem, ways that are not contingent upon what your spouse does or doesn't do.

Don't waste too much time telling yourself that this situation is unfair because your spouse continues to cheat. Additionally, don't waste time feeling sorry for yourself or mulling over how insensitive they are being to you and your needs. This is, of course, absolutely true. However, the longer you wallow in your bad feelings, the more control you allow their affair to have on your life and your peace of mind. You need to be self-determining. You need to live by your values and what you believe in your heart is right. Don't allow yourself to be defined by what has happened. Take charge of your life again. But how do you do this? What does this look like?

It looks like you taking care of yourself, perhaps even re-inventing yourself to some degree. This is the time to invest in YOU. You will need to put more energy into the things that are important to you, and feed your soul and self-esteem: your work, children, friends and family, hobbies, spiritual involvements, exercise and other interests. As hard as it might be, you have to get your feet moving and try to normalize your life.

Once you have thought of some activities that you'd like to do again (or try for the first time), you will start to feel better. This is a win-win situation because working on yourself and becoming the best you can be as an individual is something you'll need to do anyway, no matter the outcome of your marriage. Granted, it would be easier for you to be proactive about taking charge of your life if you had support and TLC from your mate. For now, you don't, and you have to pave the way yourself. I wish this weren't so, but these are the times in life where you have to stand tall, be brave and take full custody of your own life.

Refocusing on your own life provides a healthy distraction, giving your mind a break from negative thinking. If your entire focus has been the pain of the affair, it's no wonder that you have been in an inordinate amount of pain. And as you've already experienced, it is a terrible way to live.

Make a detailed list of several "healthy distractions." These should be activities that are angst-free zones for you, and just absorbing enough so that your mind doesn't stray. These activities should give you pleasure. Not sure what to do?

Dust off an old dream and make it come to life. Allow yourself some time to daydream and brainstorm. What have you always wanted to do again? Or try for the first time? Get out that bucket list and check off a few of them. Short changes in scenery and geography are refreshing to the heart and stimulating to the mind, especially when your home may not feel quite like "home" during this tough time of transition. Whatever it is, nudge yourself to do as much of the "good stuff" as you possibly can.

While you're focusing on yourself, you should also notice any time that your spouse shows interest in you or anything you're doing. This is where you can put your Sherlock Holmes skills to good use: Notice anything you do or say that yields a slightly positive reaction from your mate. Take note of it. Don't look for big changes at first; just notice the baby steps forward. Baby steps might include your spouse initiating more conversation than usual, showing interest in your daily activities, being a bit kinder or more thoughtful, calling or texting during the day, asking about your day or how you're doing, and so on. When your spouse comes closer to you in these ways, pay attention to what you're doing that's triggering those reactions.

A word of warning. If you notice small steps forward, don't use these improvements as an excuse to talk about the affair. You're not on safe ground yet.

You've already told your mate that you can't work on the marriage in any real way until the affair is over. If you bring up the affair again, it will only lead to arguments. If you want to save your marriage, arguments aren't the way to do it. If you have the need to talk about the affair, find a therapist who will support your plan, or talk to a trusted friend who believes in your marriage. Discussions about the affair with your spouse right now are a dangerous minefield. I know this takes a great deal of restraint, but I also know that fighting about the affair will make you feel bad. And you and I don't want that to happen.

You also have to give your spouse the space they need to not feel pressured by you. You should allow your spouse to initiate most conversations and interactions. You may, in turn, be responsive-friendly, kind and cordial- but let them set the tone for what happens between the two of you. This also means that you don't write love letters, angry letters, or any letters at all. Just let things be for a while.

Though you have to back away from your spouse and give them space for now, it helps tremendously to keep in mind that "a while" doesn't mean forever. People can't put major parts of their life "on hold" forever. There will come a time when something will break and a decision will be made. So, I'm not suggesting that you just lay low (in terms of trying to express yourself to your mate) for the rest of your life; I'm suggesting that you give your spouse a chance to sort through this mess and come out the other side without interference from you. As long as you are noticing small improvements, you are on the right track. This might, however, take time.

And I can hear you saying right now, "How much time?" Unfortunately, there are no universal answers to this. Just be patient as long as you can, and then some, and watch for signs that your spouse is losing interest in the affair partner. You might notice your spouse spending less time on the internet or texting. It might mean fewer unexplained absences. You may be spending more time together as a family. Once your spouse has re-invested in your marriage, you can broach the subject of working the program in this book…together.

I also want to tell you something about ending affairs. If the affair was meaningful to your spouse, even if they are willing to end it, chances are, it won't happen cold turkey. Many people end affairs in fits and starts; that is, they say their farewells, but have contact again. This happens over and over until the relationship dies a natural death. Few end affairs with a very clean break. Even if there is a clean break, typically, there is grief about ending a meaningful relationship.

As hard as this is for you to accept, it's important that you don't over-react if your spouse seems to be sad or down about the decision to part ways with the affair partner. It's normal. You have to give your spouse a chance to feel the feelings and let go, which will happen in good time. It helps if you understand that your spouse is going through a phase and eventually, it will end. If you get overly emotional about your spouse's lingering feelings, your spouse will begin to wonder if they made the right choice in calling it quits.

This is not to say that I don't expect you to have intense feelings about your spouse's reaction to the loss, I am just coaching you to either keep your feelings to yourself, or express them to people who might understand. Choose people who will support you and let you vent or cry, but not condemn your spouse. This is a natural transitional period and you will just have to have faith that, in time, your spouse's emotions about the affair will fade.

If you're someone who, after reading this chapter so far, feels you simply can't be quiet while your spouse continues to have an affair, the alternative is for you to tell them what you are going to do if the affair continues. If you feel compelled to do this, I have a suggestion.

Rather than say, "You have to end this relationship or I'm leaving," which will undoubtedly lead to defensiveness, you might consider saying, "I'm not telling you what to do. You are a grown person. You have your own needs. You get to do whatever you want to do in life. I'm not standing in your way. But I do have to tell you that I can't deal with this situation anymore. It hurts too much. It defies everything I believe in. So, if you choose to continue to have a relationship with your affair partner, I will have to _____ (move out, separate, divorce) in order to protect myself and move on with my life. The choice is yours."

Again, if you're going to go this route, be clear about what you are going to do and when you're going to do it. Be prepared to follow through with your promise. Think though all the possible ramifications of your decision. Make sure this is the path you want, given the realities of the situation.

But before you draw the line in the sand, here's something else you should seriously consider. At The Divorce Busting® Center, we have an excellent telephone coaching program. Your coach will help you come up with a specific plan to wait out the storm in your marriage. You will be supported every step of the way. It will help you feel better. And it's important that you not make a life-altering decision until you feel better and are clear-headed. Never make important decisions in the middle of a crisis.

If you're interested in speaking to an experienced, highly skilled Divorce Busting® telephone coach, you can call to schedule an appointment- 800-664-2435 or 303-444-7004, or visit my website at divorcebusting.com.

One final note. Despite your frustration about your spouse continuing to see the affair partner, I can't tell you how many couples I've worked with over the years where it seemed that one spouse would *never* give up the affair! But in time, that's exactly what happened. If your spouse is someone who seems determined to pursue the affair, it doesn't mean they'll want to be involved with that person forever. My vote is for you to hang in there and do what you can to take care of yourself in the meantime.

If, at the end of this "wait period" (however long you can do it), you feel you need to leave your marriage, you will need to strengthen your self-esteem anyway. Why not start now and get all your ducks in a row? Why not work on yourself and what you will need to make your life stable and happier again? Who knows? When you actually stop working so hard on your "marriage project," your spouse may notice, wonder what's up, and start inching their way back to you. I've seen this happen time and time again.

Here's what happened for someone who followed my advice when her husband wouldn't give up his affair. Let this be an inspiration to you!

> My husband was convinced he was in love with another woman (a co-worker) and that he didn't feel that way about me anymore. He moved out, to sort things over in his mind, and to create space and distance for us. It desperately wasn't what I wanted, but he seemed resolute that it was best.

Weeks before, I would have told anyone that we had the best, most solid marriage anyone could find. His revelation to the opposite had shocked me, and sent me reeling.

It was Mother's Day when I decided to really work on me, and start implementing your techniques. (My husband had moved out about 3 weeks earlier.) I immediately sensed a change in him. By Memorial Day, he was considering a future with me again. By July, he was ready to break off his relationship with his co-worker who he claimed to have fallen in love with 3 months earlier. By August, he had quit his job to get away from her, broken off their relationship, moved back home, and we were ready to start again. We moved to a neighboring state to get a fresh start in October. By April (for our 10th anniversary and one year after finding out that my husband was in love with another woman), he surprised me with the most wonderful, heartfelt, genuine present.

He had a minister pay us a visit during our weekend-getaway for our anniversary. The minister was there to renew our vows in a private ceremony for just the two of us. My husband wrote his own NEW vows and read them to me. It was the most amazing moment in my life and I knew then that all the doubt and worry could disappear. Everything was better -forever!

My husband and I are happier and more grounded than we've ever been in our lives. We now know how to work on issues in a positive manner, and our communication with each other is better than I ever imagined. I am so in love with my husband, my best friend, and better yet - I am certain he is with me as well. Thank you, Michele.

Now it's your turn!

CHAPTER NINE

WHEN YOUR BETRAYED SPOUSE WANTS OUT

PERHAPS WHEN YOU started reading this book with your spouse, you were both on board for trying to repair your marriage. But then, over time, your spouse- the one who's been betrayed- seems to have decided that working things out is too hard and now, they want out. Your spouse may have a strong belief that infidelity is an insurmountable wrong and cannot see a path to heal from the pain.

Many people tell themselves that they're willing to deal with all sorts of problems in marriage, but infidelity is a deal breaker. If the affair violated a basic core value, your spouse might not be able to envision ever feeling good again in your presence. It just seems overwhelming, much too painful and confusing. In their current frame of mind it seems easier to walk away from the mess, the hurt, the gargantuan job of forgiveness plus the long-term effort of healing, and beginning again. (And even with betrayed spouses who want to work things out, they will have moments of overwhelm when they feel most of the emotions above.)

Many spouses who feel that infidelity is the unpardonable offense, are often black-and-white thinkers. They believe, "Once a cheater, always a cheater." Although my work with couples has taught me that this is certainly not the case, some people refuse to believe that change can happen.

Another reason your spouse might not be interested in working things out is that the discovery itself, indeed, *the very way* your spouse learned about the betrayal, might have been incredibly emotionally damaging. For example, if you divulged the information in a piecemeal manner, leaking out a little information at a time, your spouse likely lost even more trust in your ability to tell the truth, the whole truth, and nothing but the truth. They were devastated, again and again, so that their ability to trust anything you say becomes limited. This is especially true if they begged you for the truth.

Sometimes, the realization that the lies are continuing, becomes the "point of no return," and people give up on their marriages. Betrayed spouses don't want to live their lives worrying about lies and future escapades. They prefer to cut their losses and move on.

Also, if your spouse discovered the affair on their own as opposed to your telling them about it, they might feel that, had it not been for their spying, you never would have fessed up and the affair would still be on-going. This undermines trust in a big way.

Another reason your spouse might want to end your marriage is that you haven't been doing enough to persuade your betrayed spouse to stay. Here are some mistakes an unfaithful spouse might make:

Not saying, "I'm sorry," often enough

Making apologies that don't seem sincere

Not going out of your way to comfort your hurting spouse or to reassure them about your whereabouts

Feeling impatient about the healing process

Telling your spouse that they are over-reacting instead of being empathetic

Defending your actions and making excuses for what happened

Not doing things you know your spouse wants and needs such as your being more involved with the kids, housework, flirting with him or her, finding a job, or communicating better. Your spouse may feel that you're not trying hard enough to make amends

Not being willing to commit to a new life of monogamy together if that's what your spouse needs

Being impatient with your spouse's mood swings

Continuing to flirt with or stare at other sexually attractive people

Any or all of these situations might make your spouse feel that working on your relationship isn't worth it. Additionally, if your spouse was unhappy in the marriage prior to the affair, the affair may be the final straw that broke the camel's back. Now, there may be no going back.

Regardless of why your spouse may not be interested in working on your marriage right now, if you still want to keep your marriage and family together, that should be *your* goal. That's what you should work towards. In the end, it may or may not work, but at least you're being true to your values.

If your spouse has told you the marriage over, how you respond is very important. Please do not get angry, threaten, or debate your spouse's reasons for wanting to end the marriage. You have to stay calm, and avoid being combative under any circumstances. Any bad behavior on your part- yelling, threatening, blaming, condemning, putting the kids in the middle- will be seen as evidence that the marriage isn't worth saving.

So, take a deep breath if you're given your walking papers. Tell your spouse that, given what they've been through, you can understand why they might want to leave. You must talk about the mistakes you've made and how very sorry you are. You should discuss your plan to become a better person. Be specific. For example, say, "I know I've been working long hours and not spending enough time with the kids, and I plan on changing that. I'm trying to cut back my hours at the office." Or, "I know I haven't been willing to have dinner with your parents. But I am planning to make time for getting together with them."

Your spouse will think that you are just trying to be a better person as a means to manipulate him or her, and that over time, you will stop the "good behavior" and revert back to the old you. Tell your spouse that you can understand why they might feel cautious, but being a better person- a more active parent, more mentally present when you're home, more affectionate, less critical- makes you feel better.

Therefore, you are going to continue engaging in these behaviors from now on, not just to save the marriage, but because it makes you feel better about yourself. Tell your spouse that you don't necessarily expect them to believe you right now, but this is something you know about yourself with certainty. You like the person you're becoming and you're going to stick with it, regardless of what happens to your marriage.

And then, no matter what your spouse says to you in response, even if it's disparaging, you have to take the high road and ignore it.

But what if you've tried all of the above, and your spouse stills appears hell-bent in getting out of the marriage? Here's my advice. Don't try to convince your spouse to stay by presenting convincing arguments. Convince your spouse to stay through your *actions*. Behave in ways you know your spouse appreciates, or would have appreciated in the past, before the revelations of the affair. Do these things even though you won't get any positive feedback about your actions. Just because your spouse isn't commenting about your efforts doesn't mean they aren't seeing the changes. Keep up those positive changes, even if you don't get encouragement.

Additionally, your considerate, loving actions can't last for a day, a week or even a few weeks. These behaviors have to become a way of life. What I'm suggesting that you do, can't be an act. It must be sincere and come from your heart or your spouse, whose bull-shit-ometer is already high, will sense it. But if you continue to grow, change and become a better, wiser, more considerate and loving person (and not just "perform" like one), your mate will take note. Your positive growth/changes, plus time, in a variety of circumstances, will show your spouse that your changes are real and that it's safe to let their guard down and inch their way toward trust again.

So, give your spouse space, but keep being a good person, someone who your spouse could eventually love again, someone who you are proud to be, for your own integrity. Make sure you're not doing anything that triggers your spouse's fears that you are continuing to see your affair partner. Stop spending time on Facebook if it triggers your spouse. Be accountable for your whereabouts. Don't have secret email accounts. Make your life an open book. Be trustworthy. And again, don't expect kudos or compliments. You're not going to get them for a while.

If you keep up the positive changes, and you're noticing slight improvements, then it might be time for you to test the waters to see if your spouse is open to a bit more connection and closeness.

Try sitting close together on the couch one night. Try touching his or her back or giving a short back rub. Try offering a quick peck on the cheek.

If any of these actions prompt your spouse's interest, it's clear that things are improving. So, slowly, gradually, introduce more times when you are reaching out to your spouse.

If, on the other hand, your spouse recoils when you reach out, you know what you need to do! Stop touching or testing the waters! It's too soon to be affectionate. Your spouse isn't ready to receive your advances. Just go back to being a conscientious, caring and empathetic spouse. It is my hope that, with time, you will melt your spouse's heart.

You can even try doing something I often suggest to my clients who are in your shoes. Write a heart-felt letter to your spouse, explaining all the things you believe you've done wrong, things that have hurt them deeply. Do not become defensive or explain *why* you have behaved in that way, just let your spouse know that you understand why they are struggling.

And then, at the end of the letter, tell your partner that you do not expect a response at all; you simply wrote this letter to share what has been on your mind and in your heart. Again, do not expect a letter in return from your spouse. You have to get into a place of emotional peace and strength, being truly okay with no response from your betrayed spouse. This is something you do for yourself, a gift of "owning your part" that you are giving your mate, no strings attached.

Then, after you share the letter, just move on with your life. Don't appear as if you're hanging around waiting for something to happen. That would defeat the purpose.

I have seen this letter writing exercise be very productive. It is often the first time a betrayed spouse genuinely feels that their unfaithful partner "gets it," and that their partner is willing to take personal responsibility for the ways in which the marriage has been harmed. Even if the unfaithful spouse has *verbalized* regrets about their behavior in the past, there's something different about the apologies being written in "black and white." This apology letter can break through icy emotional walls and reconnect distant and warring spouses. Let's hope it works that way for you.

But what happens, if despite your best efforts, your spouse makes it clear that he or she is moving out or wants you to leave. What do you do then? You might consider a separation.

By the way, you don't have to move out in order to separate. You could try an "in-house separation." This means that you can sleep in separate bedrooms. You can structure your lives differently so that you have less contact with each other. You can decide together how much time you want to spend as a family, couple or alone. You can have ground rules for how you interact with each other. You truly can give each other lots of space to see if this improves things between you.

If an in-house separation isn't sufficient, you might consider a physical, geographical separation. During this time, don't hover over your spouse. Give them space. Let your spouse see what it would feel like to have you around less often. If your spouse is willing, you can talk about some ground rules of separation.

A great resource to sort out all these issues is a book entitled, SHOULD I STAY OR SHOULD I GO?: HOW CONTROLLED SEPARATION CAN SAVE YOUR MARRIAGE by Lee Raffel. This book will help you think of important topics to address when you and your partner are apart.

The good news is that a separation does not necessarily mean that your marriage is over. Although I prefer couples working through their differences together, under one roof, it is also true that some couples really need a break in order to press the emotional reset button. You and your spouse may be one of them.

Don't despair if you are going to take a time out. Remember the old saying, "Absence makes the heart grow fonder?" While there are certainly no guarantees that this will be true for you, if there is too much contempt, mistrust, anger and hostility that is not lessening over time, taking a little break may not be the world's worst decision. Besides, if your spouse is determined to have a break, you might not have any choice. The goal is to make the separation as productive and marriage-friendly as possible.

I ended the last chapter by telling you about our wonderful telephone coaching program. We specialize in working with the one spouse who truly wants to make the marriage work when the other one does not. You may be finding yourself in this situation. If you are, please don't hesitate to try several coaching sessions. Not only will they offer you specific direction about what you should and shouldn't do, you will also find the coaching to be extremely emotionally supportive.

You will have to control your knee-jerk responses and doing what "feels natural," as you reign in emotions and do only the things that serve your ultimate goals. Trust me, this is not easy. In fact, it is one of the hardest things you'll ever do and many people can't do it alone.

Your coach will walk this healing path with you until the coast is clear. We have lots of success in helping 11th hour couples turn things around when all hope has faded. I'd love it if you were one of them. So, again, call 303-444-7004 or 800-664-2435. We will get you set up with a coach quickly!

Another resource I've developed to help the more motivated spouse trigger positive change in their relationship is a 90-minute video program called, The Last Resort Technique. I use this approach with many of my private therapy clients with great success. This video offers a step-by-step program to help you become an expert on what you need to do differently to get through to your disinterested spouse. When you watch it, you'll feel as if I'm in the living room with you, coaching you in concrete ways to influence your partner to reconcile.

If you're interested in purchasing this program, you can find out more about it here: http://divorcebustingtraining.mykajabi.com/.

If divorcing is looking more and more likely, you might consider attending a 2-day intensive session with me in Boulder, Colorado. The vast majority of the time, one spouse truly wants to save the marriage and the other does not. Additionally, 85 - 90% of the couples in my practice are dealing with infidelity. I have developed many tools for helping couples heal from affairs over the years. Even if your spouse is highly reluctant, we can help you find ways to broach the subject of coming to an intensive session in Boulder. So, call us and ask for information about these 2-day sessions. Again, 303-444-7004 or 800-664-2435.

The bottom line is this: if you are fighting for your marriage alone, reach out for help. Trying to restore love after betrayal can be a lonely process. You don't have to do it alone. Help is right around the corner.

Finally, you should sign up for my free newsletter which has lots of helpful information. Visit http://www.healingfrominfidelity.com to sign up!

PART V

AFFAIR-PROOFING YOUR MARRIAGE

TEN TIPS FOR AFFAIR-PROOFING YOUR MARRIAGE

I 'M THRILLED THAT you have gotten this far in the book and that you're doing the hard work to repair your marriage. I know it hasn't been easy, but I also know the payoffs are truly worth it. I hope and assume you are feeling the same way!

Additionally, I'm certain that you don't ever want to go through this painful process again. Although there are no guarantees in life, I can tell you that if you follow the advice in this chapter, you will keep your marriage strong and make it less vulnerable to serious relationship problems in the future.

My tips for affair-proofing your marriage are based on my extensive work with couples who worked through the incredibly challenging issues surrounding infidelity and now have long-lasting, loving and trusting relationships. You could say that these principles for affair-proofing your marriage have been field-tested.

Make them a part of your daily life and you and your spouse will have "love insurance."

Here they are:

1. Make sure your marriage is the # 1 priority

Don't ever take your marriage for granted. Your relationship is a living thing. If you nourish it, it thrives. Ignored, it gradually dies.

John Jacobs, M.D., wrote, "The single greatest weapon in the battle to ensure the survival of a long-term relationship is to maintain awareness of the fragility of the marital bond."

Once they have said, "I do," many couples make the mistake of thinking they've checked "marriage" off their To Do List, and after the honeymoon phase is over, their relationship goes to the bottom of the list as other things- kids, careers, education, hobbies, other friendships- start taking priority.

In our busy lives, it's incredibly easy to prioritize everything but our spouses. Although all of the above are important, and we need other interests to balance our lives, for a marriage to be successful, it must be the *most* important part of our lives. But what does this mean?

Ask your spouse.

Seriously. Ask your spouse, "What do I need to do so I can help you feel that our marriage is my top priority?" Is there anything I need to do or stop doing to show you how important you are to me?"

Then listen, absorb, and do it.

Some people tell their spouses, "I would like you to spend less time at work; and when you are home, less time on your computer." Or, "I wish you wouldn't spend so much time on your cell phone when I'm around. You can make your calls when I'm away." Or, "It would really mean a lot to me if you were equally involved in the bedtime routine with the kids. That would show me that you value our relationship." Or, "It would be great if you initiated sex more often. Right now I feel like I'm the only one interested in our sexual relationship." Or, "I know you don't like going to sporting events, but I would really enjoy having you there with me occasionally." Or, "If you would just sit next to me and watch a good movie on television once in a while, I'd feel like I matter to you." Or, "I know it may be my insecurity speaking, but I need to hear you say that you find me attractive or that I am beautiful to you. Whenever that thought flits through your mind, it helps me feel more wanted and more secure, if you verbalize these thoughts."

The key here is to truly take to heart what your spouse is saying, whether or not you agree with it. In fact, if you're having a hard time imagining yourself doing something you really don't enjoy, you need to re-read Chapter 5. In particular, read the section on the importance of doing real giving. It will give you the boost you need to take care of your spouse so that your marriage thrives.

2. Spend quality time together

When my best-selling book, DIVORCE BUSTING, was first published, I was inundated with questions from reporters about what I thought was the primary cause for the breakdown in relationships in our country. I felt certain that the reporters were expecting some sophisticated psychological explanation. But I had a simple answer. It's this.

Couples aren't spending enough time together.

Everything else in life becomes more important than sacred time together. Whether it's the kids, careers, extended family, friends, hobbies, or community commitments, marriage often gets put on the back burner. And this spells disaster for marriages.

Time together builds connection and friendship. It's a building block for intimacy and deep feelings of love. When small, irritating problems pop up, we can more easily give our partners the benefit of the doubt and let the small things slide if we are feeling connected to them. But when we're disconnected, the small, irritating things become big deals. We make mountains out of molehills. With the little time we have together, we end up wasting it by fighting.

In fact, when we don't spend enough time with our spouses, we often find we're on edge and critical of everything they do, even the "good things." For example, if a husband realizes that he hasn't been spending enough time with his wife and he extends the olive branch by bringing her flowers, instead of being truly pleased, she may think to herself, "*Gee, I wonder what he feels guilty about.*"

Time anorexia – starving for togetherness - leads to a generalized negative mindset in marriage. The fix for that? Quality time.

The phrase, "quality time," holds different meaning to different people. Some people feel connected to their spouses when they're sitting next to each other on the couch, watching television together. Others need to have intimate conversation over dinner or as they sit side by side on their deck, enjoying a glass of wine in the evening. Busy parents may feel they can't really give each other the focus they crave unless they're spending some time away from their home and children.

So, ask your spouse what quality time means to them. You need to consider *your spouse's* definition when planning time together. Remember, you don't have to agree with the definition, you just have to honor it. And that goes for both of you.

I want to stress something here. If you have children, I know it can be challenging to find time alone as a couple. But you must prioritize this. If the kids are young and need a babysitter, ask family to watch them for you. If you don't have family nearby or your family isn't a good resource, do your homework and find a reliable babysitter. If money is tight, trade off babysitting with another couple in need of free time. No excuses.

Lots of hard-working parents who spend many hours at their jobs feel it's vital to spend quality time with their children when they're home. I agree. Kids matter! But if you don't prioritize your marriage first, the children may become causalities of the tension between you in the home, and eventually the fall-out of a divorce. So, just because you have kids doesn't mean you can slack off on regular date nights. A "standing date night" once a week, or every other week is ideal. It's *that* important. And don't get hung up on who finds/gets the babysitter or who plans the date. Don't keep score. Just do it!

You can also set aside time every evening to connect after the kids go to bed. Start a ritual of taking a bath together, or having a glass of wine on the couch at some point every evening. Or if you are too tired to connect after the kids go to sleep, teach young kids to play quietly for about 20 minutes while you and your spouse have your private time together.

If the kids are used to having your uninterrupted attention, it may take some time for them to learn that their parents are temporarily off-limits. But it's wonderful to teach them the important life lesson that marriage is to be cherished.

3. Choose your battles wisely

The worst possible advice you could ever give a newlywed couple is to share your feelings with your spouse every time you're upset, disappointed, angry, annoyed, irritated or frustrated. Trust me on this one. As someone who has been married for a very long time, full disclosure of all random critical thoughts about your spouse is a formula for disaster. Frequently correcting or criticizing your mate, won't change them, and doesn't serve your goals for a better marriage.

Because no two people are alike, there will be times when your spouse says and does things that will bother you. But if you make an issue out of every small irritation, you will be fighting a great deal. Research shows that, in order for a relationship to thrive, there needs to be significantly more positive than negative input. (Specifically, there needs to be at least five positives for every negative, according to acclaimed marriage researcher, John Gottman.) The good has to vastly outweigh the bad in marriage. For the good to outweigh the bad, it often requires a willingness to overlook small irritants, take a deep breath – remember the overall positive qualities in your mate – and, if it really is a small issue, *let it go*. Our spouses need to do the same thing. Give each other a break; stop demanding perfection and look, instead for the good things they are doing. What we focus on expands. So, focus on the positives in your marriage, and the good things will begin to take on a life of their own. We need to give each other breaks. We need to be kind, compassionate and understanding.

If you are constantly nagging your mate for every little flaw, their default mode will be to go on the defense. Then, when something really big happens that you'd like to discuss, your spouse will just think, "Here we go again. What's the matter *now*?" Your issue won't be given the attention it deserves.

When you want to discuss a particular issue or concern, give it time and space before you speak. Let the dust settle. Don't strike while the iron is hot. If, after waiting for a while, you are still troubled by something that happened, then, by all means, have a conversation about it. Just make sure it's a "must discuss" topic.

And remember: timing is everything. Wait for the right moment; when you are both fed, rested and not distracted. When there is relaxed space and time to talk in the most positive way you can about a negative issue. But don't think you're being weak by letting things slide from time to time. There's wisdom in letting go.

4. Talk about what's in your heart

What I am going to say next might seem contrary to the tip offered in the previous section. Don't hold in what's in your heart. Stand your ground on important issues. Let me explain.

One of the most common patterns I see in couples whose marriages are in trouble is that one spouse has been extremely unhappy about something and yet, has said nothing about their heartache. It usually goes something like this.

In the early years of the marriage, when something hurtful or bothersome happened, the unhappy spouse broached the subject with their partner. But nothing changed; or worse, their concerns were belittled or dismissed. When their pleas for change went ignored or unheeded, the hurting spouse began to feel there was no point in addressing the issue anymore. They began to feel powerless, accepting that nothing they said or did mattered: nothing would ever be different in the relationship.

So, months pass and nothing is said about disappointments or hurts. But then, something happens and the disappointed spouse can no longer hold it inside. But instead of talking about negative feelings in a calm, constructive way, there is heightened anger which appears to be out of proportion to whatever just happened. And because the mate's anger seems so irrational, and over the top, it is dismissed. The dismissal reinforces to the unhappy spouse that there's no point in discussing matters of the heart because again, nothing ever changes.

And then the unhappy spouse goes underground with their resentment and anger. This holding back can go on for years.

Harboring resentment, anger, disappointment and hurt for long periods of time is a surefire way to destroy intimacy and loving feelings.

That's why it's important to identify when something is truly standing in the way of your feeling close to your spouse, and make sure that you talk about it. If you have difficulty sharing deep, intimate and vulnerable feelings, get help. Don't let negativity fester. Be transparent about your core emotions.

If your spouse isn't understanding the significance of what you're trying to communicate, consider this a sign that you probably need a third party- a professional therapist- to help you feel heard. Feeling misunderstood leads to loneliness. You don't want that to happen. It's too painful. You can avoid this by talking about what you need and want, even if it's hard.

Here's what one woman had to say about her marriage after healing from infidelity:

> We have come a long way. Before the affair, I thought that we had the perfect marriage, but I was blind. Although things are cheery now, I refuse to take anything for granted again. I thought we understood each other before, but realized that communication was missing. Now we really talk...about our dreams, our fears, our hopes, our future. We also talk to each other if there is something bothering us about the marriage. Previously, we thought that we should avoid this topic because in successful marriages, everything is perfect. Now we know that nothing is perfect and if things are not right, we need to talk to each other...not to someone else who "understands me."

If you have trouble talking about tough subjects, one of the best things you can do for your relationship is to learn communication skills. There is one skill in particular that many, many couples find helpful. It's called Active Listening. Many marriage educators teach this skill and you will have no trouble finding a class where you can learn it.

In short, Active Listening requires you and your spouse to take turns being a speaker and listener. After hearing one or two short sentences from the speaker, the listener's only job is to repeat back what they have heard. The listener should not comment or editorialize, just listen.

This is more challenging than it sounds because, generally speaking, when our spouses are discussing heated topics, as listeners, we are thinking about what we want to say next. But that's not really listening. This exercise helps people become better listeners. It also leads to increased understanding and compassion for our partners.

So, if you and your spouse have difficulty talking about tough subjects, find a class where you can learn this skill. You'll be so glad you did.

5. Focus on the positive

I've often noticed that it is much easier for spouses to criticize each other than it is to offer compliments. People often feel as if they're "working on their marriages" when they're telling their spouses what *isn't* working or what they're unhappy about.

But here's the truth about people. I touched on this above, but let me say it even more clearly and emphatically: the quickest, most efficient way to bring about positive change and breed good will is to catch them in the act of getting things right and bringing on the fanfare. Let your spouse know on a regular basis how important they are to you. Explain the reasons why you value them so much. Talk about what you appreciate. It doesn't matter how small their deed might be. Tell your spouse how much it means to you that they did something for you.

Take this one step further. Don't let a day pass without telling your spouse something that you're grateful for. For example, say, "I don't tell you this often enough, but I very much appreciate what a great provider you are for our family," or, "I just want you to know what a fantastic mother you are for our children and how fortunate they are to have you dedicate your life to them," or "Thanks so much for making dinner tonight, I really appreciate it," or "It meant a lot to me when you were willing to attend my work function yesterday."

You might even think about giving yourself an assignment. Make sure you compliment your spouse at least once a day. This will encourage you to keep your eyes open for anything positive that happens. Wearing positive lenses is a great way to show your love to your partner. And remember, what you focus on, expands.

6. Keep sex and passion alive

In Chapter 7, I wrote about the importance of re-energizing your sexual relationship. Once you've accomplished re-establishing intimacy, you have to keep your marriage sexy. As I told you, touch is a tie that binds. Making love, having quickies, cuddling, holding hands, snuggling on the couch are ways two people feel close and connected.

If you and your spouse feel differently about the importance of sex, it's important to re-read Chapter 7. Feeling unhappy sexually is one reason people stray. Make sure that you're doing whatever you need to do to keep your sexual relationship vibrant. But what is a sexually vibrant marriage?

A sexy marriage isn't defined by the number of times people have sex. I've worked with lots of couples who have regular sex, but one of the spouses feels it's perfunctory or obligatory. When having sex feels emotionally flat to one partner, it becomes a problem because many people tell me that *their spouse's* enjoyment is their biggest sexual turn on!

So, if you're in a long-term marriage, you have to figure out what *you* need to do to keep passion alive. Don't become complacent about sex. Keep talking to your spouse about it. Be playful. Try new things. Read a sexy book together. Buy a new sex toy. Watch a hot movie side-by-side. Send flirty texts throughout the day. Get dressed up, go to a restaurant or bar and pretend you just met. Then, test your best "pick up lines".

Check in with each other; take your sexual satisfaction temperature on a regular basis. Keep your sex life a priority.

7. Make yourself happy

I always say that relationships are the one place where one half and one half do not equal a whole. Each person has to feel good about his or her life in order for the relationship to be successful. You can't depend on someone else for your happiness. You have to wake up in the morning and enjoy what you do each day. You need to feel as if you're living your life in a purposeful manner. If you're unhappy with your choices, there's no way you can be available emotionally in your relationship. Your unhappiness will spill over into your marriage.

Unhappiness can turn into depression. Depression colors everything we see in negative tones, including each other. And studies show that depression is contagious in marriage. If one spouse is depressed, it lowers the happiness of the other.

But the good news is that there are great resources for people who aren't feeling good about themselves or their lives. Start by reading a self-help book such as, DEPRESSION IS

CONTAGIOUS, by Michael Yapko, Ph.D., or UNSTUCK, by James Gordon, M.D.. Consider seeking help from a therapist who practices a strengths-based therapy approach such as Solution-Oriented Brief Therapy. Don't forget one of the best antidotes for depression- regular exercise. Some people also benefit from supplements or even medications. It's important to remember that there are many pathways out of the darkness of despair that is depression.

But why is it so important to your marriage to feel good inside? People who are happy with their life choices have a great deal to contribute to the relationship. They want to share. They have something they're excited about. They have lots to talk about at the end of the day.

So, you need to take an inventory of what turns you on in life. Do you love your work? Do you enjoy being a stay-at-home parent? Do you derive joy from your volunteering, hobbies or the way you spend most of your time? You owe it to yourself *and* your spouse to make sure that you're living your life fully.

The more satisfied you feel with your daily routine, the more likely it is that you will be present for your spouse and the people you love. If you aren't happy with what you're doing currently, make a change. And if you don't know what it will take to increase your happiness, make the discovery of that your next project.

8. Hang out with marriage-friendly people

There's a saying, "Show me who your friends are, and I'll tell you who you are." This is true. A few years ago, there was a study that showed that divorce is contagious. It revealed that people were 75% more likely to become divorced if a friend divorced, and 33% more likely to end their marriage if a friend of a friend is divorced. In other words, we are greatly influenced by the people with whom we hang out.

The good news is that contagion works in both directions! If we hang out with folks who value marriage, love their spouses, treasure their time together, value monogamy, have strong family values and are great friends with each other, these qualities are bound to rub off on us too.

Hanging out with marriage-friendly couples might require doing a bit of grooming of your current friendships. Some may be more supportive of your marriage and the values you hold than others. If you find that your list of marriage-friendly couples is sparse, it's time to make new friends! Talk with your spouse about activities you can participate in that might lead to new, healthy relationships.

But how can you do this? Why not attend a class on improving marriages and talk to other participants? Perhaps you can find such a class at your local community college or at church or synagogue. If you can afford it, you might consider taking a couples-only cruise, going on an organized trip somewhere or taking a weekend seminar on a topic of interest to you both.

On the other hand, you might not have to do anything new at all. You may already have marriage-friendly friends with whom you have not been spending a great deal of time lately. Re-up those friendships! Invite them for dinner. Plan a fun evening with them. Dust off your old friendships and reinvest in them.

9. Commit to life-long learning

Everyone knows that relationships aren't easy. We're not born knowing how to be good partners and neither are our spouses! We learn how to "do relationships" by watching our adult caregivers when we were young. And let's face it; many of us didn't have great role models. And even if we were fortunate enough to have had fantastic parents, we might have married someone who wasn't quite as blessed. Then how do we handle the differences between us? Good question, eh?

Here's the answer. Marriage education. Marriage education comes in many forms- seminars, retreats, certain therapy sessions, coaching, and self-help books. Over the past years, we have learned so much about what it takes to have successful, healthy, loving marriages. These relationships require relationship skills, skills that can be taught and learned.

I strongly believe that it behooves couples to continue to learn new relationship skills throughout their lifetime. That's because relationships aren't static things; they're constantly changing. To make them work, you have to be flexible.

I remember when our daughter, our first child was born. We had no idea how to parent her. Over time, my husband and I found certain ways to comfort her and help her go to sleep at night. I'll never forget our first family trip with her. We drove to a cabin in northern Wisconsin, far from our home. Our car was packed to the gills with baby paraphernalia that we knew would be comforting to her in the strange environment, and therefore make our lives easier. We could hardly see out of our car windows because we packed the car so thoroughly with every imaginable baby item.

We got to our cabin, set up her crib, her baby swing and other infant equipment. And for some reason, our daughter picked *that* night to lose interest in everything we hauled with us. She hated her beloved swing. She would have nothing to do with her portable crib or her treasured pacifier. She was miserable and so were we. From that day forward, she refused to sit in her swing, even when we got home!

So, it was back to the drawing board for us. What worked like a charm during the first few months of her life was now a dreaded activity. We scratched our heads in dismay but learned a valuable lesson that night. Nothing stays the same. Life changes. What works one time doesn't necessarily work at a different time. We needed to get with the program and keep up with her changes.

So, too, with marriage. Just when you think you've got it down, your spouse changes. You change. Your needs change. Your marriage goes through transitional periods- building careers, having and raising kids, dealing with in-laws, handling financial challenges, becoming empty nesters- and so on. Don't think for a moment that your marriage stays the same as you weather these changes. You have to learn to roll with the punches.

I tell couples that people in long-term, happy marriages actually have many marriages, not just one. They must "divorce" the old marriage and remarry each other many, many times over. Each time you divorce and remarry, you create a new relationship based on what has transpired in your lives. Rebirth keeps marriage fresh.

The good news is that you don't need to reinvent the wheel each time you need or want to make a change. There are so many great resources available to couples. Take a marriage class. Read a great marriage book together. Find a therapist who teaches couples practical skills. Look at love as being a life-long learning process. Invest in your marriage. Learn how to love.

10. Don't forget to date each other

When I work with couples whose marriages are in big trouble, I always ask them to tell me how they met and what attracted them to each other in the first place. When I do, their emotions change instantly; they smile and laugh as they reminisce about the past. They say, "I just thought he was the most handsome man I had ever seen," or "She was so hot. I thought I would never get her attention." I also hear things like, "She was so accomplished and strong. I loved that about her," or "His sense of humor had me laughing all the time."

Then I ask couples to tell me about their early relationships, when they were dating. I want to know how they treated each other. Not surprisingly, most of the stories are very romantic. They were joined at the hip, spending every free moment together. It didn't matter what they did, as long as they were together. They surprised each other. They had lots of sex. They laughed. They were free spirited and did many adventurous outings. They were spontaneous. They called each other a lot. When apart, they longed for each other. They often talked about what they had in common. They snuggled, kissed, hugged. They accepted each other for who they were. They bought Hallmark cards and flowers. They talked endlessly.

You get the picture?

Although once life changes- kids, jobs, family obligations, and so on- it isn't possible to do everything you did when you were younger and dating, it is possible to reinvest energy and creativity into your marriage. I'm convinced that if people put a fraction of the energy into their marriages as they did their dating relationships, marriage therapists would be out of business! That's because new relationships feel so exciting and wonderful. Our brain chemicals contribute to intense feelings of infatuation. But I'm here to tell you that you can reproduce some of those incredible feelings intentionally.

Date your spouse!

Do romantic things. Send flirty texts. Have sex in different places. Do the unexpected. Buy flowers. Get sexy lingerie. Date regularly and go to new places. Show intense interest in your spouse's life. Look at old photos of when you met. Be affirming. Gush. Brag about your spouse in front of other people. Write love letters.

Here's a letter from a man whose wife had an affair and when they reconciled, he decided to "date" his wife.

One thing that has been a determining factor in bringing my wife and me back is a steady dating relationship. Things I would have thought of as corny or silly are now becoming general fare for our growing "new" romance. I have learned to tell her how beautiful she is first thing in the morning. I don't just *think* it (like before), I actually *say* it.

I do little things, like asking her what she wants for dinner and then ordering it for her, taking her arm when we cross the street, LISTENING to her and jotting down the things she likes and wishes for, and combing her hair at night, just to feel it in my hands and tell her how beautiful it looks. I tell her and show her every day that I love her. I don't let loving thoughts just fly through my mind without saying something.

So, go back to what worked. When you reflect on the past, there are undoubtedly some amazing clues about what you can do in the present to sustain loving feelings. Making your spouse feel special- like you did in the beginning- is the best way to keep your marriage on firm ground.

Before we say goodbye, I have some closing thoughts. On to the last chapter!

But I have one more suggestion for you before you read my final thoughts. If you'd like to watch me do a seminar for couples where I build on some of the ideas for affair-proofing your marriage that are in this chapter, check out my video training on The Marriage Breakthrough® Seminar http://divorcebustingtraining.mykajabi.com/. This training makes the tips in this chapter come alive. When you watch the seminar, it will feel like you're in the room with me! Come on in.

PART VI

AFTERTHOUGHTS

CHAPTER ELEVEN

PARTING THOUGHTS

I T'S HARD TO believe that our journey together is almost over. I want to thank you so much for allowing me into your lives and trusting me to help you make your marriage loving again. If you've followed my advice, I know you've both worked really, really hard and that it's taken a great deal of personal strength for you to have gotten where you are today. You should be very, very proud of yourselves.

I'm sure there were days when you felt like giving up…but you didn't. And you didn't give up for a great reason. You love each other. You believe in each other. You want a future together. Now, because of the hard work that you've done as you've worked through this program, growing old together is a very real possibility. Growing old together is a wonderful thing because you have a shared history and you get to keep on writing the rest of your "marriage story," with new, happier chapters to come. Part of your history is that you hit hard times, but you decided to stick it out, to work it out. That decision speaks volumes about your courage and commitment.

And speaking of commitment, I have one final suggestion for you. Why not, when the time is right, renew your vows? Why not have some sort of personal ritual that will honor and commemorate the journey you've been on together? Pick a special place and decide who will be invited to attend. Will it be just the two of you? Or will you ask others to witness your amazing accomplishment?

Then decide what you will say to each other. Think about the special promises you will make. Think about the words that will be indelibly imprinted on each other's minds as you move through the rest of your lives together.

And here's one more thing. You need to tell me about your success! You must write and tell me how you've turned things around in your marriage. There's nothing that thrills me more than to hear about people's marital triumphs. You can reach me at Michele@divorcebusting.com In the meantime, I'll be in my office waiting to hear from you and cheering you on. Goodbye, my friend.

RECOMMENDED READING

Chapman, G. *Five Love Languages: How to Express Heartfelt Commitment to Your Mate.* Chicago: Northfield Publishing, 1995.

de Shazer, S. *Clues; Investigating Solutions in Brief Therapy.* New York: W.W. Norton & Co 1988.

Glass, S. *NOT Just Friends: Rebuilding Trust and Restoring Your Sanity after Infidelity.* New York: Free Press, 2002.

Gordon, J. *Unstuck: Your Guide to the Seven-Stage Journey Out of Depression.* New York: Penguin Press, 2008.

Gottman, J.M. and N. Silver. *The Seven Principles for Making Marriage Work.* New York: Crown, 1999.

Love, P., and J Robinson. *Hot Monogamy: Essential Steps to More Passionate, Intimate Love-making.* New York: Penguin Books, 1994.

Nelson, T. *The New Monogamy: Redefining Your Relationship after Infidelity.* New York: New Harbinger Publications, 2013.

Raffel, L. *Should I Stay or Should I Go?: How Controlled Separation Can Save Your Marriage.* New York: McGraw-Hill, 1998.

Springs, J. A. *Can I Forgive You?: The Courage to Forgive, The Freedom Not To.* New York: Harper, 2004.

Stosny, S. *Living and Loving After Betrayal: How to Heal from Emotional Abuse, Deceit, Infidelity and Chronic Resentment.* New York: New Harbinger Publications, 2013.

Weiner-Davis, M. *Divorce Busting: A Revolutionary and Rapid Program for Staying Together.* New York: Simon & Schuster, 1992.

Weiner-Davis, M. *The Divorce Remedy: The Proven 7-Step Program for Saving Your Marriage.* New York: Simon & Schuster, 2001.

Weiner-Davis, M. *The Sex-Starved Marriage: Boosting Your Marriage Libido.* New York: Simon & Schuster, 2003.

Weiner-Davis, M. *The Sex-Starved Wife: What to do When He's Lost Desire.* New York: Simon & Schuster, 2008.

Weiner-Davis, M. *Getting Through to the Man You Love: The No-Nonsense, No-Nagging Approach for Women.* St. Martin's Press, 1999.

Yapko, M. *Depression is Contagious.* New York: Atria Books, 2009.

ADDITIONAL RESOURCES

The Last Resort Technique Video
    http://divorcebustingtraining.mykajabi.com/

The Marriage Breakthrough® Seminar Video
    http://divorcebustingtraining.mykajabi.com/

Divorce Busting® Telephone Coaching
    healingfrominfidelity.com

Two-Day Personal Intensives with Michele Weiner-Davis
    800-664-2435 or 303-444-7004
    Virginia@Divorcebusting.com

Made in the USA
Middletown, DE
04 February 2022